Prisoner to Patriot

Prisoner to Patriot

Copyright © 2013

ISBN: 978-0-578-12424-7

Cover photo by Susan Latos

Cover Photoshop by David Mastick

All photos by Susan Latos/Shimokochi family unless otherwise credited

Edited by Lamont Antieau

Contents

Acknowledgements   4

Illustrations   5

A Note From Nob   7

Introduction   9

Chapter One – Nob   13

Chapter Two – Was it a case of national security or something more?   25

Chapter Three – Camp #1: Santa Anita Racetrack   38

Chapter Four – Camp #2: Heart Mountain   50

Chapter Five – Freedom!   67

Chapter Six – Onward   79

Chapter Seven – Happy Endings   84

Appendix – List of camps   90

References   92

Acknowledgements

We would like to thank our generous donors. Without your help, completing this project would have been a difficult task. Thank you:

Christopher Marold

Julién Godman

Ellen and Deb Fedon-Keyt

David Nefesh Mittelman

Tim Parker-Smith

Victoria Webb Korsak

Lorraine Weber

Paul D.

Tasha Lord

Mindy Schwartz

Maureen Riley

Christine Rietz

Sharon Walsh

Sara Rodell

David Bendert

Gary Vanek

Josh Howard

R. Edgar

Chris Schultz

Andrea Kelley

Caren Hunter

Aimee Visperas

Olivia McLaughlin

Cherlyn

Tana Tapson

Sonya Mastick would like to thank Nob; along with her family, friends and husband, David.

Illustrations

Figure 0.1 Photograph of Nob and his sister, Yuri, in their school uniforms

Figure 1.1 Photograph of George's family home in Hiroshima

Figure 1.2 Photograph of Shimayo as a little girl

Figure 1.3 Photograph of George, Shimayo, Yuri and Nob in 1929

Figure 1.4 Photograph of Nob, Yuri and Shimayo

Figure 1.5 Photograph at L.A. Farmers Market

Figure 1.6 Photograph of L.A. Produce Market Wholesale in the 1930s

Figure 2.1 Photograph of a soldier with a Springfield rifle
Figure 3.1 Photograph of a replica of a Heart Mountain Guard Tower

Figure 3.2 Map of American concentration camps

Figure 4.1 Shimayo, George, Nob, and Yuri

Figure 4.2 Block 28 mess workers

Figure 4.3 Heart Mountain Hospital/Boiler Building

Figure 4.4 Map of Heart Mountain Relocation Center

Figure 4.5 George, Nob, and Shimayo

Figure 4.6 Photograph in Heart Mountain of the Shimokochi and Watanabe Families

Figure 4.7 Belt, patches, and pin from Troop 333 Boy Scout Uniform

Figure 4.8 Photograph of plaque commemorating Boy Scout Troop 333

Figure 4.9 Photograph of plague at Heart Mountain Interpretative Learning Center

Figure 5.1 Photograph of plaque commemorating Heart Mountain military inductees

Figure 5.2 Image of Army 7th Infantry logo

Figure 5.3 Image of Google map of the route from Seno to Hiroshima

Figure 5.4 Photo of Risaku Shimokochis home in Japan.

Figure 6.1 Photograph of Nob at Heart Mountain

Figure 6.2 Plaque commemorating Heart Mountain as a National Historic Landmark

Figure 6.3 Heart Mountain Sign

Figure 6.4 Photograph of Anna and Nob at Heart Mountain

Figure 7.1 Nob on his 83rd birthday

Figure 7.2 Anna, Annie, Jimmy, Sue and Nob

Figure 7.3 Great-grandson Kaelen and Nob

Figure 7.4 Photograph of Nob's family in June 2011

A Note From Nob

The original intent of this book was to convey to my children David Kiyoshi, Kenneth Noboru and Susan Anne Latos, the heritage rich in values established during the Meiji Era (1867-1912) that my father brought with him from Hiroshima, Japan in 1905. I feel it is my duty to pass to my children as it was to my father to pass it on to me. While I have the skill to document and the memories of the years, I do not have the training, skills or experience to publish a book. I am extremely grateful to the author, Sonya Mastick, and to all of those who made cash contributions without which my ambitions would not come to fruition.

The core values of the Japanese value system are shame and honor. When a couple gets married, their mission is to raise a family of children who will bring honor to the family, clan and village. Shame will bring dishonor to the same people.

The following are some of the items in the Japanese value system:

Achievement

Ambition

Appreciation

Attention to detail (quality of work)

Attitude (positive)

Commitment

Deference (show of respect)

Delayed gratification

Education (path of achievement)

Endurance (pain and difficulty)

Etiquette (show of respect)

Faithfulness and loyalty

Harmony (others over self)

Honesty – Japanese are "super honest". Lost and founds are everywhere. Finders are not keepers. No looting after disasters. Dishonesty is shameful.

Humility – It's built into the language.

Inculcation- Teaching through repetition

Integrity – Resist temptation.

Love and kindness – Filial piety. (oya koko)

Mental toughness

Obedience -show respect and positive attitude.

Patience – Tolerance

Self restraint/Self control

Self Denial (sacrifice)

Struggle – Keep trying-nothing comes easy

Tolerance – Moderate dislikes

A couple of these Japanese words do not translate to English very well. My friend Kaz Shiroyama uses the acronym "EGGGS":

Gaman – is a noun for "Gaman" endure pain, discomfort – Stoicism – Patience/opposition of short temper – Mental toughness- delayed gratification – resolve to reach a higher level.

Gambaru – is a verb for ambition-achievement-perseverance-"do or die-never quit-struggle/persevere/persistence with confidence- resolve to reach a higher level.

Anecdote:

My mother never learned to speak English fluently. Japanese was spoken at home. I learned English from the neighborhood kids; mainly Mexicans. By the fourth or fifth grade I had the ambition to want to score the highest but the Jewish kids had the language advantage. In the mean time, English had become number one and Japanese number two. This became a problem as our Japanese skills were so limited.

Introduction

Nobuyuki "Nob" Shimokochi was born on November 13, 1928, in Los Angeles, California. Born as the second child and only son of George and Shimayo, had a relatively typical American childhood: he played with the neighborhood kids, studied hard, and worked after school with his older sister and only sibling, Yuri, in the family business. The Shimokochis lived in Boyle Heights for the first nine years of Nob's life. Later his family would move to the 2300 block of South Central Avenue, a mostly black and low-income neighborhood where George had his general store, Sun Market.

Although their children were born and raised in the United States, George and Shimayo were American immigrants who had both been born in Hiroshima, Japan. George arrived in the U.S. in 1905 and Shimayo in 1924, but regardless of the length of time they had lived in America, they were not allowed to become naturalized citizens or own land, as Japanese descendants could not do so until 1952. These same rules, however, did not apply to European immigrants. So George and his wife were keenly aware of how they were viewed by some in the country that they now called home, but they remained focused on their goal of a prosperous future. Because of their Japanese values, overcoming adversity was not a new concept or challenge for them. The Shimokochis, like many American families, worked hard, paid their taxes and dreamed of a prosperous life. Being business owners, they were an integral part of their neighborhood.

Figure 0.1 Photograph of Nob and his sister, Yuri, in their school uniforms

So, given Nob and Yuri's status as American-born citizens protected by the U.S. Constitution and the legality of George and Shimayo's residence in the country, how was it possible that the Shimokochis could end up in a concentration camp on American soil?

The answer to this question is Executive Order 9066, which was put into effect by U.S. President Franklin D. Roosevelt on February 19, 1942. Under this order, the U.S. military began to round up Japanese people living in Arizona, California, Oregon, and the state of Washington, and incarcerated them in prisons. Below is the exact text of Executive Order 9066:

EXECUTIVE ORDER 9066 — February 19, 1942

WHEREAS the successful prosecution of the war required every possible protection against espionage and against sabotage to national-defense materials, national-defense premises, and national-defense utilities, as defined:

NOW, THEREFORE, by virtue of the authority vested in me as President of the United States, and Commander in Chief of the Army and Navy, I hereby authorize and direct the Secretary of War, and the Military commanders whom he may from time to time designate, whenever he or any designated Commander deems such action necessary or desirable, to prescribe military areas in such places and of such extent as he or the appropriate Military Commander may determine, from which any or all persons may be excluded, and with respect to which, the right of any persons to enter, remain in, or leave shall be subject to whatever restrictions the Secretary of War or the appropriate Military Commander may impose in his discretion. The Secretary of War is hereby authorized to provide for residents of any such area who are excluded there from, such transportation, food, shelter, and other accommodations as may be necessary, in the judgment of the Secretary of War, of the said Military Commander, and until other arrangements are made, to accomplish the purpose of this order. The designation of military areas in any region or locality shall supersede designations of prohibited and restricted areas by the Attorney General under the proclamations of December 7 and 8, 1941, and shall supersede the responsibility and authority of the Attorney General under the said Proclamations in respect of such prohibited and restricted areas.

I hereby further authorize and direct the Secretary of War and the said Military Commanders to take such other steps as he or the appropriate Military Commander may deem advisable to enforce compliance with the restrictions applicable to each Military area hereinabove authorized to be designated, including the use of Federal troops and other Federal Agencies, with authority to accept assistance of state and local agencies. I hereby further authorize and direct all Executive commanders in carrying out this Executive Order, including the furnishing of medical aid, hospitalization, food, clothing, transportation, use of land, shelter, and other supplies, equipment, utilities, facilities, and services.

This order shall not be construed as modifying or limiting in any way the authority heretofore granted under Executive Order 8972, dated December 12, 1941, nor shall it be construed as limiting or modifying the duty and responsibility of the Federal Bureau of Investigation, with respect to the investigation of alleged acts of sabotage or the duty and responsibility of the Attorney General and the Department of Justice under the Proclamations of December 7, and 8, 1941, prescribing regulations for the conduct and control of alien enemies, except as such duty and responsibility is superseded by the designation of military areas hereunder.

February 19, 1942 – Franklin D. Roosevelt

Rather than being based on facts, the controversial order was given during a post-Pearl Harbor panic that swept the nation in the aftermath of the Japanese bombing of Pearl Harbor. At the heart of the order were bigotry and ignorance, much of which was based on a long tradition of fear of Asian people, whose ethics, looks and value system were very strange to other Americans. Highly contested by many Americans and even members of the United States government at the time, the order went to extremes in a country that had already historically been oppressive to Asians, granting the government authority to administer preemptive incarceration without due process and for an indefinite period of time. What seems to be the most dangerous aspect of the order is that it is as vague as the tools of war and racism often are. (As a side note, President Obama signed into law H.R 1540 on December 31, 2011, authorizing the same conditions. The new law again uses the term "concentration camp." The new concentration camps will be administered by FEMA instead of the WRA [War Relocation Authority] (govtrack.us.)

What this ultimately turned out to be, in the eyes of the government, was a sweeping act designed to capture any spies or traitors living closest to Hawaii, and it only affected people in the western states. Whereas one would think that it would be especially important to concentrate on the location of the Pearl Harbor attack, Hawaii, almost all of the Japanese people living in Hawaii were exempt from this rounding up of mostly innocent people. Nearly 40% of the population of Hawaii in 1942 was Japanese; however, when the government wanted to put them into internment camps, the wealthy farm owners strongly objected. At this point, the sugarcane crops were a major source of income for not only the Hawaiian farmers but for the country as a whole. Thus, the plantation owner weren't defending the Japanese people so much as they were defending their crops, as the bulk of their cheap labor was done by the Japanese (pbs.org).

Despite being one of the ugliest parts of American history, strangely, in most people's minds, World War II and Executive Order 9066 or concentration camps are not synonymous. Even when they are expressed in layman's terms as an "internment camp," many people look confused, as if this couldn't have happened on American soil. Reactions seemingly range from vague recollection to flat-out denial. To take this notion even further, the history books cover this dark period in American history with the same lack of candor and honesty as they do when discussing the treatment of Native Americans or slavery. Even among those who actually lived through the period are many who would like to forget it or rebuff the severity of the situation. It is discouraging and disheartening at times to look back at the heart of a nation that was buried in hatred and fear, but it is indeed important to look back. Not only to honor those who were affected by the heinous actions these prejudices produced, but to see just how we as Americans arrived in such a place and vow to never return in the future. Never again should we rule out common sense over fear or the misunderstanding of another culture.

However, as surprising as it might sound, Nob is neither bitter nor angry about his experience. Rather, he seems to take it all in stride with detached wisdom and a mild manner. Interview after interview revealed a man with loyalty to the United States as shown through his service in the military, an undying love for his family and a great supply of opportunities that he created for himself by merging his life in the states with the Japanese virtues instilled in him by his parents. The life of Nob Shimokochi has been a captivating and unpredictable one, but it serves as a shining example of how virtue and faith can steer a ship though any storm.

Chapter One
Nobuyuki Shimokochi

Nobuyuki, whose name in Japanese means "one who performs or acts out of faith", was born to Mr. Tamesaku "George" Shimokochi and Mrs. Shimayo Shimokochi, both of whom were from Hiroshima. Shimokochi is about as close to a spelling translation of this surname as could be ascertained according to the Hepburn System, which was named after its founder, James Curtis Hepburn. Developed around 1887 to help Romanize the spelling of Japanese names of people who came to America, the system has since been revised and is now called Hepburn Romanization (see judopedia.com). In addition to essentially being forced to Americanize their names, Japanese immigrants were also encouraged to convert from the religion of Buddhism to Christianity.

Born in 1889, George Shimokochi arrived in the United States in 1905 to make additional money for his family, with the intent of only staying in America temporarily. Today, it is difficult to imagine a 16-year-old child arriving in another country to make a living on his own, but these were different times, and such choices were often made out of sheer desperation. At the time, Japan was suffering a massive famine due to a failed rice crop, and so Japanese families were sending their second-born sons to build more prosperous lives elsewhere and to aid their families by sending money back home.

> "A year before George came to the United States, his father told him to go to a mission where he would get shelter, food, religious instruction along with learning how to read and write in English," says Nob. "He became what is known as a 'mission boy', and churches played an important role in recruiting Japanese immigrants. I remember that my father had beautiful handwriting and I would think that the missions helped with that."

A popular term for the first-born son in Japan is Ichiro (as well as Kazuo, among others). The Ichiro is the "favorite", a practice that is better known as Agnatic Primogeniture, which is often just a cultural tradition, but in many places is accepted as actual law: "The Global Property Guide notes that most Japanese citizens do not write wills, relying on the Japanese Civil code to uphold the rules of primogeniture. The Japanese Family Registration System provides detailed documentation on all family relationships, indicating the proper heir for most inheritance situations" (Norman).

14

In the case of Agnatic Primogeniture, the first-born sons are entitled to all of the estate once the parents die and are given the responsibility to disperse the assets in a manner they see fit. First-born sons in Japan were also favored by girls searching for a husband for obvious reasons of security and a husband who would be able to provide in the long run. In cultures that honor the system of the oldest male inheriting everything, his value is of the utmost importance in assuring the family heritage and lineage for the future. He is to care for his parents and all assets pertaining to the parental estate. Since the second-born son (known as Jiro in Japanese) assumes far less responsibility under such a system, he is often sent off to make money for the family. In his case, George was the first-born son, and since it was a rarity in Japanese culture to send the first-born off, his story is a unique one in and of itself. Although Nob really couldn't say why his father was sent off, he did state that

> "There were four boys, and three of them went off to the States at some point or another. Maybe in this way they weren't bound to tradition? Of the brothers who came to the States, Uncle Shimaji was the intellectual one and became an activist who worked for the rights of the working man. When he went back to Japan, he wasn't regarded too well by the government because of his activist status. They put him in prison. When he eventually got out, he married. In addition, he was a newspaper journalist abroad and a graphic artist. Uncle Shigeru had six kids and not only came to the States as well, he ended up staying permanently. Youngest brother was Itsuichi, [who] stayed in Japan, never once visiting the States."

Even after more than ten years in which he established a good, quality life in the United States, George kept in close touch with his family in Hiroshima, making trips back to Japan when he could. Like most parents, George's mother and father wanted him to find a suitable mate and start a family, and he too was starting to long for a spouse since he was now in his early thirties.

> "In Japanese culture, family plays a heavy role in selecting the bride," says Nob. "If the family is having

difficulty finding a good lady, they would even hire
somebody to search for her. There was very little divorce
because the selection wasn't so emotional. Many
Japanese families at this time had mostly arranged
marriages. If the man was already in the States, the
families would send photos back and forth."

In 1907, Theodore Roosevelt and the Japanese Consulate General reached
a "gentleman's agreement" in which Japan would cut back on their
immigration. However, most of the Japanese immigrants at the time were
men, and they needed/wanted wives of Japanese descent, so further
negotiation on immigration policy was of great importance to the
American government. Because many of the Japanese men who worked
in America were in Hawaii, the plantation owners thought it would help
them retain their staff if they could get them married and settled down in
Hawaii. This started the trend of "picture brides." As many people know,
this was a popular movie but for those who haven't seen it and don't
understand its premise, here is the long and short of it. Many families in
Japan (along with Korea and China) used a Nakodo or a "go between"
who would take the men's photos that were submitted and try to find a
wife for them. At this point the families would inform the Nakodo what
they were seeking as suitable criteria on behalf of the potential bride and
groom. The things that were considered desirable in women for their sons
varied from family to family but essentially included things like age, the
bride's family's wealth, health, beauty and whether the family had an
honorable surname. There were many motivations for the women to
participate: poverty, family pressure, the lure of freedom in the states,
down to the simple popularity of their friends doing it. Whatever the
reason it was very popular for a time. But we are digressing here…

George wasn't going to have an arranged marriage per se; instead, his
family was one in which the parents heavily influenced not only who their
children would ultimately marry, but who they would even get a chance at
meeting with the possibility of marriage. It was indeed his family, and not
a Nakodo, that arranged a meeting for George to meet Shimayo, who
would end up becoming his new bride, although it would not happen
entirely according to tradition.

Figure 1.1 Photograph of George's family home in Hiroshima

Shimayo was born November 10, 1905, and she was from the same village as George: Kami-Seno-Cho, Akigun County, Hiroshima. This village was situated in a very rural area and, along with most Japanese culture at that time, romance did not play a part in the courting process there. As members of George's family were searching their village for a mate for him, Shimayo caught wind of this and saw a picture of George. After seeing his picture, she became unusually forward about marrying George because she thought he was good looking and kind and was certain that she wanted to marry him. However, George's family did not consider Shimayo a first choice because she was 16 years younger than him. Although it was uncommon in Japanese culture at that time for women to be so forthright with their wishes, Shimayo fought for George and eventually won. This made their love story unique, and one that was told around the village for years. This story was retold to Nob by a cousin, and he expressed how grateful he was to know the real story of his parents' meeting.

Figure 1.2 Photograph of Shimayo as a little girl (app. 1908)

Shimayo and George were married in May of 1924, when she was 19 years old and George 35. They were married twice: once in Hiroshima and later in the United States. With their nuptials behind them, it was time to make a decision: would they stay in their hometown or would they go to live in George's home in California? George thought that he could make a better life for them in America, since he was already established there. At this point, he had already lived there longer than he had lived in Japan, and, while he loved his village, he knew it would be best to not stay but head back to his other home instead. However, almost immediately a dark cloud was cast over their new happy nuptials when they almost missed the deadline to enter and live in the United States because of a new law enacted May 26, 1924. This was the Johnson-Reed Immigration Act, which limited the time that immigrants could live in the States (procon.org).

Shimayo was a devoted wife and mother.

> "She was very giving and always sacrificed for our
> family," Nob fondly recalls with a soft smile on his face.
> "That generation of women were especially known to be
> very giving and I think she was exceptionally above and
> beyond her generation. She was a wonderful mother who
> instilled in us with the ability to excel. She only spoke
> Japanese, so she couldn't help us with our homework
> because it was all in English, not to mention she only had
> a sixth-grade education. However, through her character
> and teaching she set us up with not only the ambition
> but the desire to do well."

When Nob was four, the 1932 Summer Olympics were in Los Angeles,
and he remembers his mom telling him that Japan excelled in many events
in the Olympics and that, in spite of being such a tiny country, they made
a large impact on the world stage. He took that lesson with him
throughout his life. Because of the deep respect he had for his mother,
Nob doesn't remember rebelling much as a teenager nor did Nob's own
kids: "I think that has a lot to do with respect. If it is instilled in the child
to have respect, he's not going to be rebellious."

During all the reminiscing about his mother, Nob recalls a story where he
felt his mother went above and beyond to make him feel loved and cared
for. "My mother and I were eating toast but only mine had jam on it," he
says. So noticing the difference, he asked her, "'How come you don't have
jam on your toast?' She replied, "Oh, I don't like jam.'" However, he
knew that they were so poor that there was only enough for him. When
speaking of his mother, Nob often uses the phrase *kodomo no tame ni*,
which means "for the sake of the children." The Japanese people often
explain their sacrifices as if it were the only natural thing to do.

Figure 1.3 Photograph of George, Shimayo, Yuri and Nob in 1929

Nob's older sister and only sibling was named Yuriko Shimokochi. She was born in 1925. The English translation for Yuri was "Lily," but she never liked that name and simply went by Yuri. She eventually married Max Koga and had one child, Jon Koga. "She was a hard worker, smart, and very proper but a bit more Americanized than myself," says Nob. Nob and his sister were known as Nisei, which means "second generation" but were the first-born generation in the states. Nob spoke mostly Japanese until the third or fourth grade, when English became the primary language of his sister and him. They both learned a great deal of English by simply playing with the children in the neighborhood. He explained that while education was difficult up until he spoke English, it didn't stop him from getting good grades and, more importantly, competing with the other students for the best grades. "They seem to make a big deal about language these days, but we got along just fine and learned easily out of necessity," says Nob. It was paramount for Japanese children to bring their parents honor by earning good grades and doing the best job they possibly could at all things. Nob confesses that he didn't exactly "excel" with his grades but did the best he could.

Figure 1.4 Photograph of Nob, Yuri and Shimayo

The very first company that George was part owner of in the United States was the L.A. Farmers Supply Company, where he was a partner in the early- to mid-1930s. George fell into the job due to the illness and eventual death of a previous partner, Mr. Miyomoto. In an odd twist of fate, some years later, Nob met Mr. Miyomoto's daughter, Aiko Anna Marie Miyomoto, who got in touch with Nob after seeing an article written about him. "She said she read my story in the paper about attending the dedication of the interpretive learning center and tracked me down," said Nob. They discussed their fathers and the connection of their families through the company.

Figure 1.5 Photograph at L.A. Farmers Market (Yuri, holding the doll; Iko; Clair; and customers)

The company sold agricultural goods such as insecticides, fertilizers, along with tools and horse-drawn cultivators/plows. To meet the many agricultural needs there were at the time, there were numerous stores like George's in Los Angeles, and many were Japanese owned. Nob's earliest memories are of being with his father while he would make his early morning rounds trying to make sales at the produce market where all the farmers would offer their produce for sale to the grocery stores.

Figure 1.6 Photograph of L.A. Produce Market Wholesale in the 1930s

Upon recalling this time, Nob says, "I remember the produce was so impressive. The celery and peaches were huge. They all looked so fresh and vibrant." After that, his father would take Nob with him to the flower market to try to make some sales there as well. Nob beams when he speaks of his father taking him at the young age of six or seven years old to work. While his dad made daily runs to the produce and flower market, Nob could only go on Saturdays, but listening to him speak of this time of his life, one gets the feeling that Nob would have enjoyed being with his father at work every day of the week.

It was in this part of the interview that Nob wanted to be clear about his feelings for his father, "He was great! He was a little on the permissive side as he would let us get away with a lot of stuff. He was well respected by the community, a leader in the church. I think my mother was proud of him because everybody thought he was such a great guy."

Eventually Nob's father purchased the Sun Market in 1937. It was essentially a mom and pop store general/grocery store. (Even though they were not wealthy by any means, George was able to travel back to Japan several times, which put him under suspicion of the American government.)

During this timeframe, a man was hired to help out in the store named Thomas Robinson, who, it should be mentioned, was black. Maybe it was because they were considered outsiders, or it was out of just plain decency, but Nob's family treated Thomas like family, and in return, he felt like part of the family. Nob sadly remembers how lost Thomas felt the day that all the Japanese people just seemed to have vanished. And to think what it must have been like for an all-Japanese business to hire a black man during the 1920s. Nob stayed in touch with him his entire life, until Thomas passed away in 2011. Upon his death, an article was written about Thomas in which he spoke warmly of the Shimokochis, detailing their relationship and how he even called Nob's parents *mamasan* and *papasan*. Nob recalls:

> "He took to the Japanese culture and learned the language. He could not only speak it but could also write it. He was friends with mostly Japanese people even at school…he was a good man. He was a school psychologist and his wife was a librarian at a university.

My wife and I would stay with him from time to time while visiting California. The last time I saw him, I brought him some sushi that he really liked."

The Shimokochis were well liked, their store a prominent figure within the community, and their lives were good. They were living the American dream, but all of that was about to suddenly change.

Chapter Two

Was it a case of national security or something more?

Before we can talk specifically about the evacuation, it seems important to understand why Nob thought that this happened, as well as to learn more about a history of U.S. and Japanese relations from his perspective. It is not just Nob's contention, but rather, it is a popular belief among many different races of Americans that the overall blind hatred for Asian people was at the root of this event and that it started when the Chinese were making their way to the United States for the Gold Rush, more specifically, the California Gold Rush, which started in 1848. This is clearly shown by the rapid increase in Chinese in California:

> "At the beginning of the year 1849, there were in [California] only fifty-four Chinamen. At the news of the gold discovery a steady immigration commenced which continued until 1876, at which time the Chinese in the United States numbered 151,000 of whom 116,000 were in the state of California" (Norton 283).

It is easy to see that when money is involved, tensions will arise, but to be fair, the Chinese weren't the only ones capitalizing on this windfall of money. It was a cash cow for anybody who was daring enough, had the proper funds to make the journey and was willing to do the hard work. So why were the Chinese singled out for such hatred? As is often done even in modern times, the media strongly played a role in telling the American people how they should feel about the Chinese. Because their clothing, religion and culture were so different from white America, the media tried to portray them as unclean, inferior and even as evil people (The Chinese Experience). Nob says:

> "During the Gold Rush time period, the Chinese were treated so poorly that they reported the behavior and specific activity to the Chinese consulates. However, the hatred was so strong that even the consulates could do nothing to curb the anti-Chinese and in turn the anti-Asian sentiment."

Because of this, things did not look good for any Asians moving to America.

When asked if he thought this backlash was mostly about money because at the time Asians would work for far less money and were largely far more productive, Nob conceded that was of course part of it but the overall theme was about their specific race.

> "It was a strong racial thing. America was for the whites and not for the Asians. That Asians came over was considered a threat that Americans called the Yellow Peril – 'a danger to Western civilization held to arise from expansion of the power and influence of eastern Asian peoples – Merriam-Webster,'" said Nob. "At the time [Asians] were an enigmatic people who had strange values and beliefs."

Some would have said that even Americans felt that that the Japanese belief system was stronger. Nob lays out some of the basic principles:

> "There are values like Gaman and Ganbare that every kid knew. Gaman means to endure pain or discomfort, to be patient, delaying gratification which in turn provides the individual with mental toughness. Respecting your elders was non negotiable. Teachers, known as Kyoshi, were addressed as Sensei. This was also a title reserved for doctors, professors and teachers. Teenagers rarely ever rebelled against their parents and you wouldn't dream of causing trouble at school. If a conflict was to arise at school, you might bring disgrace (known as Haji in Japanese) to your family and with that, you would also face stern disciplinary action from your father."

It is fair to say that even to current day, the Japanese culture is very different from that of the Western world. Nob is quick to point out that Japanese values are instilled so deeply and across the board that even in a crisis they would not disgrace their family name:

> "There is a difference between Japanese honesty and American honesty. When there is an earthquake or other natural disaster, American looters descend on the victim's homes and businesses like vultures attacking a

carcass even with the National Guard patrolling, but the Japanese looters did not appear at the disaster sites. There was a case in point when the power failed in a Japanese supermarket and it closed but the people in the checkout line returned the next morning to pay for the food they took home."

The value system, in a spiritual sense, is a combination of Buddhism, Shintoism and Taoism (which is actually Chinese but has heavily influenced Japanese as well).

"It's not just a religion, but it's built right into their behavior pattern, their language, and becomes their culture," says Nob. "Even though many Japanese people consider themselves Christians, those other religious value systems are deeply ingrained into their culture."

One example of this is a sport that most Americans are at least somewhat familiar with: sumo wrestling. Most of the rituals performed throughout a sumo wrestling match are symbolic to aspects of Shintoism:

"To begin with, the sand that covers the clay of the dohyo is itself a symbol of purity in the Shinto religion. And the canopy above the ring (yakata) is made in the style of the roof of a Shinto shrine. The four tassels on each corner of the canopy represent the four seasons, the white one as autumn, black as winter, green as spring and red as summer. The purple bunting around the roof symbolizes the drifting of the clouds and the rotation of the seasons. The referee (gyoji) resembles a Shinto priest in his traditional robe. And kelp, cuttlefish, and chestnuts are placed in the ring along with prayers for safety" (sumotalk.com).

Thus, the country's most popular sport promotes and reinforces religion. This is just one of many examples of culture, entertainment and daily life enmeshing seamlessly with the religious beliefs of the Japanese.

As mentioned in the Introduction, the Japanese were encouraged to change their religious beliefs from whatever they were to Christianity, which in most cases meant converting from Buddhism. Christianity was just one of the many ways the U.S. government tried to Americanize the Japanese. For the U.S., it must have been perplexing having forced an entire race of immigrants into changing their last names and religion, while not being successful in their attempt to change their deeply held beliefs. The U.S. did not understand that religious faith was in fact the basis of the entire culture and could not be changed so easily. And this is where most believe the clash of cultures originated. The Japanese could not be watered down or molded into American ideals of what an American should behave like nor look like, but they were indeed becoming Americans, like it or not.

Let's be clear though: it isn't as if the Asian belief system is perfect. One of the negatives of having a deeply ingrained belief system that includes such beautiful values as harmony and honor is that is also includes ones such as Tatemae, which means never wanting to say anything that would displease someone in a conversation. Nob used the example of the 2011 tsunami in Japan:

> "A perfect example of this was during the Tsunami when the nuclear power plant had a melt down. They didn't say anything about the meltdown because they didn't want to upset people."

He said that it was possible that the operators of the facility were hiding it for scandalous reasons but was more convinced that they simply didn't want to displease the people or the government. Clearly, this is a problem because it affects the world. "Sometimes they just omit the whole truth," says Nob. "Technically they aren't lying, but they don't want to displease you with the whole truth." Another thorn in the belief system is in what some could perceive as an overly intense pride felt to be associated with all Japanese surnames. Nob referred, for example, to the Balloon Boy fiasco that played out in the media for weeks in 2009:

> "Three days after the world watched a giant balloon fly through the air as a tearful family expressed fears that their 6-year-old boy could be inside, authorities announced what millions suspected: The whole thing

was staged" (cnn.com).

As Nob remembers, because the mother of the child discussed in this story had a Japanese first name, "she brought shame to her clan" and on Japanese people in general. This is indeed vastly different from the American value system.

Whether the Japanese belief system was considered to be an asset or hindrance by the Japanese people, the U.S. government didn't want any part of it regardless. While they did everything they could think of to make the Asians more American as a whole, for example, by encouraging them to disown aspects of their culture and heritage, by making them appear different and evil to the American public, which, in turn, still considered them a threat. Nothing confirmed this belief more than the bombing of Pearl Harbor.

Nob takes a long poised breath before saying, "The war broke out when I was in the 7th grade and that's when we were terrorized by the FBI." Nob was 13 and his sister Yuri 17 on 12/7/1941, which President Franklin D. Roosevelt called "a day which will live in infamy." For Nob and Yuri, this was the day that their lives would change forever, as soon they would be informed by radio and local postings that they would have to leave their homes. Here is the actual evacuation order that was posted in the Shimokochi's neighborhood.

WESTERN DEFENSE COMMAND AND FOURTH ARMY
WARTIME CIVIL CONTROL ADMINISTRATION

Presidio of San Francisco, California
May 3, 1942

INSTRUCTIONS
TO ALL PERSONS OF
JAPANESE
ANCESTRY

Living in the Following Area:

All of that portion of the City of Los Angeles, State of California, within that boundary beginning at the point at which North Figueroa Street meets a line following the middle of the Los Angeles River; thence southerly and following the said line to East First Street; thence westerly on East First Street to Alameda Street; thence southerly on Alameda Street to East Third Street; thence northwesterly on East Third Street to Main Street; thence northerly on Main Street to First Street; thence northwesterly on First Street to Figueroa Street; thence northeasterly on Figueroa Street to the point of beginning.

Pursuant to the provisions of Civilian Exclusion Order No. 33, this Headquarters, dated May 3, 1942, all persons of Japanese ancestry, both alien and non-alien, will be evacuated from the above area by 12 o'clock noon, P. W. T., Saturday, May 9, 1942.

No Japanese person living in the above area will be permitted to change residence after 12 o'clock noon, P. W. T., Sunday, May 3, 1942, without obtaining special permission from the representative of the Commanding General, Southern California Sector, at the Civil Control Station located at:

> Japanese Union Church,
> 120 North San Pedro Street,
> Los Angeles, California.

Such permits will only be granted for the purpose of uniting members of a family, or in cases of grave emergency.

The Civil Control Station is equipped to assist the Japanese population affected by this evacuation in the following ways:

1. Give advice and instructions on the evacuation.

2. Provide services with respect to the management, leasing, sale, storage or other disposition of most kinds of property, such as real estate, business and professional equipment, household goods, boats, automobiles and livestock.

3. Provide temporary residence elsewhere for all Japanese in family groups.

4. Transport persons and a limited amount of clothing and equipment to their new residence.

The Following Instructions Must Be Observed:

1. A responsible member of each family, preferably the head of the family, or the person in whose name most of the property is held, and each individual living alone, will report to the Civil Control Station to receive further instructions. This must be done between 8:00 A. M. and 5:00 P. M. on Monday, May 4, 1942, or between 8:00 A. M. and 5:00 P. M. on Tuesday, May 5, 1942.

2. Evacuees must carry with them on departure for the Assembly Center, the following property:

(a) Bedding and linens (no mattress) for each member of the family;

(b) Toilet articles for each member of the family;

(c) Extra clothing for each member of the family;

(d) Sufficient knives, forks, spoons, plates, bowls and cups for each member of the family;

(e) Essential personal effects for each member of the family.

All items carried will be securely packaged, tied and plainly marked with the name of the owner and numbered in accordance with instructions obtained at the Civil Control Station. The size and number of packages is limited to that which can be carried by the individual or family group.

3. No pets of any kind will be permitted.

4. No personal items and no household goods will be shipped to the Assembly Center.

5. The United States Government through its agencies will provide for the storage, at the sole risk of the owner, of the more substantial household items, such as iceboxes, washing machines, pianos and other heavy furniture. Cooking utensils and other small items will be accepted for storage if crated, packed and plainly marked with the name and address of the owner. Only one name and address will be used by a given family.

6. Each family, and individual living alone, will be furnished transportation to the Assembly Center or will be authorized to travel by private automobile in a supervised group. All instructions pertaining to the movement will be obtained at the Civil Control Station.

Go to the Civil Control Station between the hours of 8:00 A. M. and 5:00 P. M., Monday, May 4, 1942, or between the hours of 8:00 A. M. and 5:00 P. M., Tuesday, May 5, 1942, to receive further instructions.

J. L. DeWITT
Lieutenant General, U. S. Army
Commanding

SEE CIVILIAN EXCLUSION ORDER NO. 33.

9

It was at this time that the Japanese were informed that they were going to be rounded up and sent away. Nob remembers the specifics, "They told us to bring bedding, toiletries and whatever else we thought we needed. I mean really, how were we to know what we needed?!" The authorities told them to bring the "essentials," and "We had to bring only what we could carry." Small children couldn't really carry much, so it was up to the adults to bring what they could. Some of the memories are faint, but Nob still recalls that his family brought mementos and family photos along with some other household items.

Being a good businessman and knowing they would have to leave, George liquidated everything and sold the business. When asked if his father had ever thought of not surrendering and to instead flee with the family, Nob replied, "No, no not a chance. There was litigation by about three or four people to avoid detainment but that failed." Alas, there was no due process and the people were rounded up anyway.

At this point, the family was told to move to Japan Town or Little Tokyo, where everyone would be rounded up and taken to the American concentration camps. (The people who didn't fit into a specific zone were greeted at their homes by Army trucks filled with men armed with bayonets and were taken to a camp.) The meeting point was at their church, Japanese Union Church, which was on San Pedro St. in Los Angeles and ironically stood in the shadow of city hall. Because money was tight, three churches merged together to make up Japanese Union Church. When asked why his father conceded to moving before being rounded up Nob replied, "My father wanted to leave with his church friends." They stayed at the church for a couple of weeks before leaving. Nob and the other children played games and found things to do to occupy their time. They weren't nearly as alarmed about where they might be going as the parents, and the adults sought to not worry them about the details.

> "We had been there for a while, so we did what we could to kill time. Being Japanese in Japan Town, there were several bathhouses where the whole family could go. Many families would go there to relax and later back at the church the kids would play games with friends," says Nob.

But the day finally arrived when the government posted the evacuation notice to a utility pole on the corner of First Street and San Pedro. The order was issued in San Francisco from the headquarters for the Western Defense Command by General John L. Dewitt. Dated May 3, 1942, the order said the evacuation was to take place on May 9th, a mere six days from the day the order was posted to evacuate the church! One has to wonder if it was done so quickly to avoid people fleeing the country. Here is a portion of the order:

This is a portion of Lt. Gen. J.L. DeWitt's letter of transmittal to the Chief of Staff, U.S. Army, June 5, 1943, of his *Final Report; Japanese Evacuation from the West Coast 1942.*

1. I transmit herewith my final report on the evacuation of Japanese from the Pacific Coast.

2. The evacuation was impelled by military necessity. The security of the Pacific Coast continues to require the exclusion of Japanese from the area now prohibited to them and will so continue as long as that military necessity exists. The surprise attack at Pearl Harbor by the enemy crippled a major portion of the Pacific Fleet and exposed the West Coast to an attack which could not have been substantially impeded by defensive fleet operations. More than 115,000 persons of Japanese ancestry resided along the coast and were significantly concentrated near many highly sensitive installations essential to the war effort. Intelligence services records reflected the existence of hundreds of Japanese organizations in California, Washington, Oregon and Arizona which, prior to December 7, 1941, were actively engaged in advancing Japanese war aims. These records also disclosed that thousands of American-born Japanese had gone to Japan to receive their education and indoctrination there and had become rabidly pro-Japanese and then had returned to the United States. Emperor-worshipping ceremonies were commonly held and millions of dollars had flowed into the Japanese imperial war chest from the contributions freely made by Japanese here. The continued presence of a large, unassimilated, tightly knit and racial group, bound to an enemy nation by strong ties of race, culture, custom and religion along a frontier vulnerable to attack constituted a menace which had to be dealt with. Their loyalties were unknown and time was of the essence. The evident aspirations of the enemy emboldened by his recent successes made it worse than folly to have left any stone unturned in the building up of our defenses. It is better to have had

this protection and not to have needed it than to have needed it an not to have had it – as we have learned to our sorrow.

3. On February 14, 1942, I recommended to the War Department that the military security of the Pacific Coast required the establishment of broad civil control, anti-sabotage and counter-espionage measures, including the evacuation, therefrom of all persons of Japanese ancestry. In recognition of this situation, the President issued Executive Order No. 9066 on February 19, 1942, authorizing the accomplishment of these and any other necessary security measures. By letter dated February 20, 1942, the Secretary of War authorized me to effectuate my recommendations and to exercise all powers which the Executive Order conferred upon him and upon any military commander designated by him. A number of separate and distinct security measures have been instituted under the broad authority thus delegated, and future events may demand the initiation of others. Among the steps taken was the evacuation of Japanese from western Washington and Oregon, California and southern Arizona. Transmitted is the final report of that evacuation.

5. There was neither pattern nor precedent for an undertaking of this magnitude and character; and yet over a period of less than ninety operating days, 110,442 persons of Japanese ancestry were evacuated from the West Coast. This compulsory organized mass migration was conducted under complete military supervision. It was effected without major incident in a time of extreme pleasure and severe national stress, consummated at a time when the energies of the military were directed primarily toward the organization and training of an Army of sufficient size and equipment to fight a global war. The task was, nevertheless, completed without any appreciable divergence of military personnel. Comparatively few were used, and there was no interruption in a training program.

6. In the orderly accomplishment of the program, emphasis was placed upon the making of due provision against social and economic dislocation. Agricultural production was not reduced by the evacuation. Over ninety-nine percent of all agricultural acreage in the affected area owned or operated by evacuees was successfully kept in production. Purchasers, lessees, or substitute operators were found who took over the acreage subject to relinquishment. The Los Angeles Herald and Express and the San Diego Union, on February 23, 1943, and the Tacoma News-Tribune, on February 25, 1943, reported increases not only in the value but also in the quantity of farm production in their respective areas.

7. So far as could be foreseen, everything essential was provided to minimize the impact of evacuation upon evacuees, as well as upon economy. Notwithstanding, exclusive of the costs of construction of facilities, the purchase of evacuee motor vehicles, the aggregate of agricultural crop loans made and the purchase of office equipment now in use for other government purposes, the entire cost was $1.46 per evacuee day for the period of evacuation, Assembly Center residence and transfer operations. This cost includes financial assistance to evacuees who voluntarily migrated from the area before the controlled evacuation phase of the program. It also covers registration and processing costs; storage of evacuee property and all other aspects of the evacuee property protection program. It includes hospitalization and medical care of all evacuees from the date of evacuation; transportation of evacuees and their personal effects from their homes to Assembly Centers; complete care in Assembly Centers, including all subsistence, medical care and nominal compensation for work performed. It also reflects the cost of family allowances and clothing as well as transportation and meals during the transfer from Assembly to Relocation Centers... .

Lt. Gen. J.L. DeWitt to the Chief of Staff, U.S. Army, June 5, 1943, in U.S. Army, Western Defense Command and Fourth Army, *Final Report; Japanese Evacuation from the West Coast 1942,* Washington D.C.: Govt. Printing Office, 1943, pp. vii-x.

The order outlined the districts that were being evacuated by chopping up the state into zones; every so many days a zone would have to go. Not everybody had to leave together to get transported to the camps, nor did all the remaining get rounded up at home, but in fact, many people arrived in their private vehicles.

> "They came in their own cars and trucks. There were immediately impounded and stored into the infield of the track. They were not allowed to sell them. Cars and tires were at a premium because all of these items were no longer in production for civilians and were being used for the war only. But they were burnt!! Set on fire!" says Nob. "Now my dad put our family car in storage because we didn't know how long we would be there, and

because it was so long, we defaulted on the payments and lost it."

It seems that the country was hell bent on destroying the Japanese people's existence then and well into the future. Many theorize that the U.S. Government wanted to make it so unbearable for Japanese to live in the states that after their detention, they would just pack up and move back to Japan. To give an idea of the monetary impact, "Since the families were forced to move very quickly, they were forced to sell what they couldn't take at low prices, generating losses estimated at billions of dollars" (freeinfosociety.com).

Saturday, evacuation day arrived, and the staging area was in the parking lot of the church. A large bus pulled up with its windows covered. There was a squad of soldiers in WWI uniforms, armed with rifles and bayonets. "It was a shock," says Nob. "It meant surrendering to soldiers with actual weapons." The soldiers carried WWI issued Springfield rifles, as shown below.

Figure 2.1 Photograph of Soldier with a Springfield rifle

Compared to modern-day rifles, the Springfield rifle looked crude and not unlike a BB gun rifle but were weapons that could kill if need be. What made them visually menacing were their fixed bayonets. "On command, we dropped our bags, and they motioned us onto the bus." Nob remembers with a somber look on his face that the women were trying to stifle their tears, along with those of their children. Suddenly they were prisoners of war, but Nob is quick to point out the government's reluctance to use the words "prisoner of war":

> "They wouldn't use the word P.O.W. because that has connotations they didn't want. Under the Geneva Convention, there's a standard of how to treat prisoners, and they didn't plan to adhere to it."

By its very definition prisoners of war do not have to be soldiers but can be nonmilitary people captured by an army and held against their will. When the order came out, it addressed all of the Japanese people as alien or non-alien. Despite being born in the United States, Nob wasn't considered a citizen but a non-alien.

On May 9, 1942, Nob stepped onto the bus, and there were already people on board. Watching the women choke up made Nob emotional. When asked how he felt, he simply said,

> "Very insecure. The shades were pulled down, so no one in town could see the government driving us away, but I lifted the shades to sneak a peak on the drive. Who knew if I was ever going to see this place again?"

And just like that, when the bus was full, the refuges were sent on their way to Santa Anita Racetrack, which was located near Pasadena. This would be the location of their first concentration camp and, sadly, their home for the next four months.

Chapter Three
Camp #1: Santa Anita Racetrack

On December 25, 1934, the Santa Anita Racetrack in Arcadia, California, opened to great fanfare:

> "A crowd of 30,777 filled the new grandstand on opening day. The next day's Los Angeles Times reported that scores of celebrities including Al Jolson, Clark Gable and Will Rogers 'rubbed elbows at the new track.' But as the early days became decades, it was the horses and their companions who became the celebrities that made Santa Anita endure" (followinghorseracing.com).

At that time, the Santa Anita Racetrack was considered an architectural gem with a flashy art deco style. And one of its most famous residents had been a horse named Seabiscuit, winner of the Santa Anita Handicap in his last start in 1940.

Two years later, in 1942, racing at Santa Anita was suspended due to World War II. This was the same year that the racetrack was converted into use as a Japanese-American internment center with prisoners taking up residence in horse stables at the track, including a then-unknown actor named George Takei. A statue of Seabiscuit stood on a court of the same name at the racetrack, and it was not uncommon for the Japanese prisoners to pose in front of the statue for photographs (Santa Anita Park, georgetakei.com).

Upon the arrival of the Shimokochis at the horsetrack, Nob recalls that the first emotion that swept across the entire population "was the shock of being prisoners of war and the dread of getting assigned living quarters." The first people who arrived were sent to horse stalls that reeked of horse feces and urine.

> "There were no utensils to even clean up the horses' mess," says Nob. "So they were loaned some cooking utensils from the kitchen to at least scrape clean the area of debris but it didn't help with the odor."

Luckily, Nob's family arrived later and ended up in the barracks. While inadequate and makeshift, they at least didn't have to deal with the wretched stench of the horse stables. Just imagining the smell of the urine soaked stalls and the sense of violation is enough to make anyone feel depressed. The Santa Anita camp was meant to be temporary until the prisoners were given permanent accommodations at other camps, and very little preparation went into making transient camps like this even remotely hospitable.

Immediately after their arrival to the camp, armed personnel took them to their assigned rooms in an army truck. During the drive, Nob noticed all the horse statues and remembers even seeing the Seabiscuit statue "life size." The camp was divided into seven zones, or districts, in all, and Nob's family was assigned to barracks in the northeast corner of the camp, which was better known as District 7. Each barrack was divided into six rooms with a family in each of the rooms and flimsy, cracked walls separating the rooms. There was no rhyme or reason to assignment – it was simply first come, first serve. Nob remembers the rooms of the barracks being very small with a single light bulb hanging in the center of the room. In addition to the poorly made walls separating families, family members only had newspapers along with sheets between the beds in their own quarters to create some privacy from one another. Because they were ordered to only bring what they could carry, they had no furniture, so they sat on their belongings to buffer them from the ground. To add to their degradation, there was no plumbing and no prefabricated beds, just army cots, and they were instructed to make their bedding out of hay. "They dropped a bale of hay and a muslin bag. We stuffed the bag and that was the bedding," says Nob. These things, along with toilets that were not in their barracks but in the latrine and had no partitions, were just part of the shocking treatment inflicted on a people who had done nothing to deserve it.

THE LAY OF THE LAND

There were 18,719 people interred at the Santa Anita, and there were 6 mess halls varying in sizes to feed the prisoners. Each mess hall was given a color name: Yellow, Red, Blue, Orange, White, or Green. Nob's was Yellow. Nob laughs, "We often waited for the Yellow Mess to open." For a young boy, the jokes at the expense of that name were surely plentiful (colorado.gov, Santa Anita (detention facility)).

Within the camp, prisoners could move freely, but they were assigned specific mess halls, with each one feeding from 3,000 to 4,000 people at a time. Responding to the question of whether or not everyone always got fed, Nob said, "Yeah. But in the beginning somebody would look at his meal and say, 'Oh, I don't like that' and not eat; but that would be the last time he did that!" They were given a ration of one teaspoon of sugar a day.

"At breakfast if you left your coffee cup upside down because you were half asleep you got a teaspoon of sugar for whatever you wanted but if you flipped your mug up, somebody would come and put a teaspoon of sugar in it and coffee, then you didn't have sugar for your cereal and there wasn't sugary cereal then. Some of it tasted like cardboard, so if you were half asleep and accidently flipped your mug up, you were stuck with cereal with no sugar and coffee. What kind of kid wants coffee?!" laughs Nob.

Even though they were fed, the prisoners were taken advantage of at every turn. One of the major issues that arose with respect to the mess halls was that some of the white people working in them would steal food:

"They would steal bacon, butter and other items. They would sell it on the black market and have no trouble getting good money for them because everything was being rationed during this time," says Nob. "But they were eventually caught."

A riot almost broke out because some of the detainees planned on stopping the car of the suspected crooks, but it never reached that point.

It's hard to believe anyone would steal the food considering how little was spent on it for each detainee.

"The WCCA (Wartime Civil Control Administration) had the same allowance prescribed by the Army – 50 cents per person per day. The assembly centers actually spent less than that – an average of 39 cents per person per day. The outside community pressed the government to cut expenses even more" (Personal Justice Denied 142).

Nob points out, "It was a common belief that treating us bad was patriotic. That only the non-prisoners got the best."

The latrines at the camp drained into a cesspool and would often overflow. When this did occur, the overflow would run underneath the barracks. This happened quite often. For some prisoners, the latrines were too far away and were a humiliating experience due to their lack of privacy. To help accommodate some of the elderly, children, and even some of the people who simply didn't want to walk such a distance to use a restroom in the middle of the night, chamber pots became a sacred possession for those who could procure them.

The shower building was about three blocks away, and the showers were actually designed for horses. Workers built a temporary, feebly constructed wall in the middle to separate the men and the women. It's easy to imagine the indignation one could feel in this situation. At times, some of the women complained that men were climbing over the walls to watch them shower, but this complaint fell on deaf ears. "When the women complained… a camp official responded, 'Are you sure you women are not climbing the walls to look at the men?'" (Hersey).

The laundry facility was a couple blocks away, which made carrying laundry heavy work, so children's wagons were borrowed to get the laundry there. Once there, the clothing was washed in large galvanized tubs.

"The women had to use the old fashioned scrub-boards," says Nob. "It was back-breaking work just to get the laundry to the laundry area and the act of cleaning the clothes was just as difficult. The entire family went and if one of the kids had to go the latrine, their mother would take the child while the father kept their spot in the line. Depending on the day, weather and what you were waiting for you could wait up to a half hour to get anything done. Everything required a long line and oftentimes it was a very hot wait! Everything was communal!"

These obstacles along with many other things, including a strict curfew, were shocking and mentally difficult to adjust to. Just weeks prior to their round up, these people, who were guilty of only being Japanese, were able to come and go as they pleased. They could sleep in their own beds, eat when and what they wanted, and stay out late at night. In other words, they could live as free citizens. Now, as prisoners, the mental dexterity to adjust to the new environment was beyond intense. But they tried to be strong and resourceful with what they had. Nob gives an example:

"The ground was often muddy and we wanted a pair of shoes for the showers so we took two-by-fours and made clogs or what we call getas. These really helped to get around camp."

While it was easier for the older children and adults to adjust, it was much more difficult for the babies.

"The government provided milk station's set up all over the camp and the mothers were issued milk every four hours around the clock. However if their children were hungry before those four hours, that was just tough luck. Some nights you could hear several different babies crying while you were trying to sleep. It wasn't the easiest," says Nob.

The women and families did what they could to keep the baby happy until the station opened again. With that being said, someone had to man the station around the clock. If a prisoner got up in the middle of the night for milk or to use the latrine, the spotlight would follow him or her there and back. The light was blinding, and all of the prisoners knew that the spotlight was directly attached to a guard tower that housed armed military personnel.

Figure 3.1 Photograph of a replica of a Heart Mountain Guard Tower

The lights would sweep over the camp, reminding its inhabitants that they were prisoners. "It was hard enough being in a different location and having hay beds, making it difficult to sleep, but having these bright flashing spot lights in your eyes made the conditions worse," Nob remembers. While to some that was scary and intimidating, to others it provided an opportunity for having a little fun. Nob laughs, "Some of the kids would play hide and seek with the men at the spotlights. They would duck behind buildings or try to outrun it for fun." Many of the children were not nearly as affected as the adults by camp life and treated it as a fun camping experience at times. But at the end of each day, like so many, Nob couldn't help but have questions:

> "Lying on this muslin-filled bed with the searchlights going, I was just puzzled. I wondered why if the Constitution and Bill of Rights is supposed to protect our civil rights, then what am I doing here? Something just isn't right! I'm 13, and these kinds of questions are new to me, very heavy. Even today when I see the word constitution or bill of rights, I connect it with the words 'concentration camps.' It still puzzles me."

In order for the camps to run efficiently many of the prisoners were assigned jobs, but bear in mind they were paid very minimally. Nob's father, George, was a census-taker, and he would check the barracks every night at curfew. The job wasn't simple nor was he very popular for doing it, but in keeping with Japanese tradition, nobody would voice their displeasure to him about it. Nob's 17-year-old sister, Yuri, had a job in the mess hall. Getting a job was important for prisoners, as with their earnings, they could order items from the Sears Roebuck Catalogue and make their lives and those of their loved ones more comfortable.

Nob's mother wasn't drafted for a job because Nob was a minor, and therefore she was allowed to care for him instead of taking up a duty. Many of the prisoners had jobs making army camouflage netting for the U.S. military, and they ultimately made over 22,000 nets for the army (Santa Anita (detention facility)). http://encyclopedia.densho.org/Santa %20Anita%20%28detention%20facility%29

One of the constant sources of irritation was the barracks checks. Every Monday the Japanese had to place all of their belongings on the ground in front of the door for inspection. The military police would come by and confiscate anything they deemed could be used as a weapon, including saws, kitchen knives, straight razors for shaving, building tools, etc. What Nob's family and the others found frustrating was that some of the items confiscated were the very items they were encouraged to bring. In addition, it appeared as if the rules changed weekly, and there appeared to be neither rhyme nor reason for what could stay and what would go. It was frustrations like these that eventually resulted in riots.

One detainee documented his experience of one such event:

> "…I saw a riot involving two or three thousand people.
> It had started when the Santa Anita officials distributed a
> list of contraband articles: hand irons, knives larger than
> four or five inches, AM radios. Well, one day the army
> came through and started to inspect the barracks for
> contraband articles, and people really got up in arms
> about this invasion of privacy. Before we knew it, there
> was a full-scale riot, and the military police, complete
> with jeeps armed with machine guns, came in to put it
> down" (Leaving Home).

In this riot and in many other instances, detainees were killed for varying reasons. In these events, along with many others, they were reminded of the seriousness of the situation and how unjustly they were being treated.

> "We found out that we were supposed to be getting a small allowance of two or three bucks a month for things like toothpaste, soap and stuff like that, but we weren't getting it" says Nob. "Somebody else was. We were supposed to be ordering from a Sears Roebuck and Montgomery Wards catalogue, but it was already too late."

The people were already stripped of so much and for no reason. With that, enough was enough. It was this justified uprising that eventually put an end to the weekly inspections.

Not everyone went willing to the camps, as some were actively fighting this detention. Mitsuye Endo (a Japanese woman) filed a petition for Habeas Corpus to plead her case of illegal relocation and wrongful dismissal, as she was a state of California employee who had been fired with the activation of the Executive Order. Not only was she fired, but it had also been declared that she would not to be reinstated if and when she got out of the camps. Endo, along with three other separate cases, contested this decision and won; however, the decision was turned over much too late, and everyone was already imprisoned by then.

Along with the rest of the prisoners, Nob and his family lived at Santa Anita for approximately four months, from May 9 to Sept 1, 1942. Santa Anita was a temporary camp, and everyone waited with anxious anticipation of learning what was to come and where they would ultimately end up. There appeared to be no real order or understanding as to who would be sent to what camp. The only thing they knew for certain is that the day would come when they had to leave, and it would be by train. The date of their departure was posted and announced in advance.

Relocating the Japanese to their permanent camps was a long and tedious task that would end up taking roughly eight months in total. In order to assure a smoother transition than there had been to the temporary camps, there were lead groups of prisoners who went before the mass population comprising doctors, teachers, labor workers, etc. They went on the first trains to the permanent camps and set up shop, so to speak.

Nob and his family were among nearly 19,000 people heading by train to their next camp in Wyoming: Heart Mountain. Heart Mountain would in fact be "home" to the Shimokochis for the next two-and-a-half years. Along with 17 other locations in California, Oregon, Washington and Arizona, Santa Anita was known as a "Civilian Assembly Center." Heart Mountain along with nine other camps was known as a "Relocation Center," which was just a euphemism for concentration camp (see Appendix for entire list).

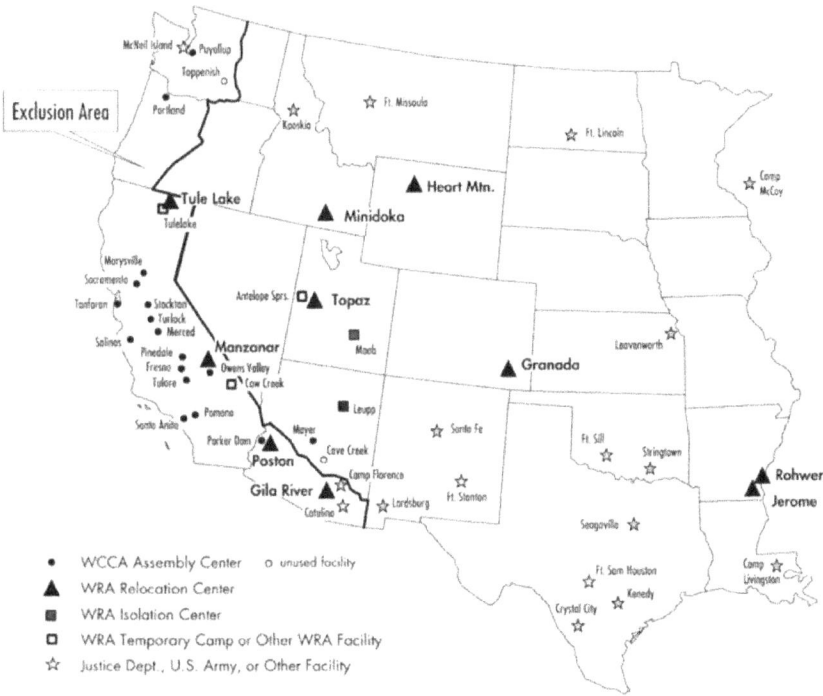

Figure 3.2 Map of American concentration camps (Burton et al. Chapter One)

In addition to the Japanese camps, there were eight Justice Department detention camps and U.S. Army facilities for some Germans, Italians and Japanese people as well. There were also three Citizen Isolation Centers that mainly held "problem inmates" (Japanese-American Internment

Camps). Just as only the best food was reserved for nonprisoners, the same sentiment went for travel and comfort. At the time, there was so much military traveling by railway, including weaponry, soldiers, steel, etc., that they had to use very old cars for the transport of the camps' prisoners. The old steam trains held about 500 people, which meant many trips had to be made to transfer prisoners from the assembly centers to the concentration camps. The trains came directly next to Santa Anita. It was so close to the barbed wire fences that the other detainees would wave goodbye to the folks leaving before them. During that day and age, train and bus travel was not as easy as it might seem, and this was especially true for the prisoners:

> "When President Franklin Roosevelt declared that all of the Japanese Americans in the selected areas were to be kept in concentration camps, trains and busses began transporting thousands of people to and from camps. These train and bus rides lasted for several days. As a matter of organization, families were given tags with a different number on them for each family. People were required to wear a tag with the number corresponding to their bags" (Eleni).

Their luggage was kept in holding areas before they were put onto trains and were searched. They, like their luggage, were treated like numbers. Something to be sorted, inspected, counted and then tagged.

On the announced day of departure, everyone was rounded up barrack by barrack. Then they were loaded onto the train with their only possessions being what they could carry in hand. For many people, especially children, train rides are an enjoyable experience. There is often a sense of adventure associated with travel by train and the experience of exploring the country one picturesque town at a time. However, for prisoners of war, it was a rough three-day train ride on a very old train.

During the ride, prisoners were seated in coach carts, so there was no place to sleep or even recline. Just as they were housed in Santa Anita in inhospitable horse stalls, they were provided about the same comfort on their way to their next camp. The train would stop once in a while to get more water for steam. By 1927, most steam locomotives were outfitted with tenders that carried water, allowing trains to travel further between stops for water, but again, prison transport was only done via old and decrepit trains.

> "The MPs would allow us to get off the train to stretch our legs when they refueled or needed more water," recalls Nob. "[However,] there was a dining car for us to eat at and the waiters were all black. This struck me as being ironic that minorities had to serve imprisoned minorities. Maybe not fully understanding the situation, they were complaining that they weren't getting tips from the detainees."

The spokesman for Nob's car was a minister who was one of the pastors at Nob's church, Japanese Union Church. He was stuck in the middle between prisoners who had no money to pay for service and waiters who felt they were being taken advantage of. This was shaping up to be a long three days. In spite of the complaining, service went on per usual, and Nob, his family, and their fellow prisoners finally made their way to their permanent concentration camp at Heart Mountain.

Chapter Four
Camp #2: Heart Mountain

In 1942, the governor of Wyoming was Nels H. Smith. When asked how he felt about Japanese internment camps being placed in his state, he responded that he not opposed the Japanese being sent there, but said if they were that "they would be hanging from every tree" (Mackey).

However, despite Governor Smith's inflammatory rhetoric, the residents of the nearest towns of Powell/Cody didn't oppose the camp, and the Heart Mountain Internment Camp opened on August 12, 1942, without incident (World War Two – Japanese Internment Camps in the U.S.A).

Figure 4.1 Shimayo, George, Nob, and Yuri

It was also in September of 1942 that the Shimokochis arrived. Nob vividly remembers his first impressions of the camp:

> "When the train entered the camp in 1942, it stopped at a little shelter that was called Vocation. I never understood why it was called that. There was nothing around there, and the train couldn't stop every five miles. Hardly anybody lives around there, and there is no town called Vocation."

However, the camp's location was chosen specifically for that reason. It was in the middle of nowhere and away from the residents of the nearby towns.

Even more startling than the camp's isolation to many of the detainees was that they arrived just in time to experience a massive snowstorm! Keep in mind that prisoners like the Shimokochis were mostly from climates that were warm throughout the year, and that; in addition, they were asked to only bring what they needed from home to the first camp. How in the world could they have imagined that they would end up somewhere that had snowstorms?! Nob recalls:

> "Even today I remember how daunting the snowstorm
> appeared because we didn't even own winter jackets
> being from California, nobody had the clothing or were
> used to a snowstorm with winds gusting up to 60 mph.
> We had a lot of buying to do and very little money!"

For those who did not have one of the camp jobs back at Santa Anita and didn't have money to purchase anything from the Sears catalogue, one could imagine that the first days at Heart Mountain were intolerable. The weather was just one of the many hardships that the detainees had to overcome, as life at all of the camps in general was very difficult.

> "The U.S. internment camps were overcrowded and
> provided poor living conditions. According to a 1943
> report published by the War Relocation Authority (the
> administering agency), Japanese Americans were housed
> in 'tarpaper-covered barracks of simple frame
> construction without plumbing or cooking facilities of
> any kind.' Coal was hard to come by, and internees slept
> under as many blankets as they were allotted. Food was
> rationed out at an expense of 48 cents per internee, and
> served by fellow internees…" (Siasoco and Ross).

To add insult to injury, there was a flu epidemic going around when the prisoners first arrived at Heart Mountain, and a doctor was there "giving you the ahhh flashlight test," says Nob. Prisoners remarked to each other about awful their surroundings looked. Nob's description of the startling transition from sunny California to Heart Mountain was that "Everything was desolate and barren looking for as far as the eye could see. It was all sagebrush and tumbleweeds." But despite the look of the grounds, he notes that "the barracks were nicer...insulated, bigger and brighter, in my opinion things were looking up." Nob recalls that some of the other children must have felt the same way:

> "To make the best of the situation many of the kids went sledding on pieces of building material down a hill just outside the camp. They got in trouble with the MPs because they were outside of the campgrounds. When we first arrived, the camp wasn't completely built. While the prisoners pitched in to get their shelters finished, they refused to put up the barbed wire."

All the barracks were arranged in blocks, and Nob's family lived in Block #28 on the northwest corner of the camp. Every 300 people had their own mess hall, latrine, showers and laundry.

Figure 4.2 Block 28 mess workers

There was a hospital, and some barracks were used for schools.

Figure 4.3 Heart Mountain Hospital/Boiler Building (2011)

That left barracks needed for supplies, the camp's administration and the guards. Nob laughs:

> "I thought it was a huge improvement over Santa Anita, if you can put a nice spin on a concentration camp. We were no longer eating with thousands of people and sleeping in horse stalls. I think Santa Anita was a conditioning event so that we could enjoy Heart Mountain."

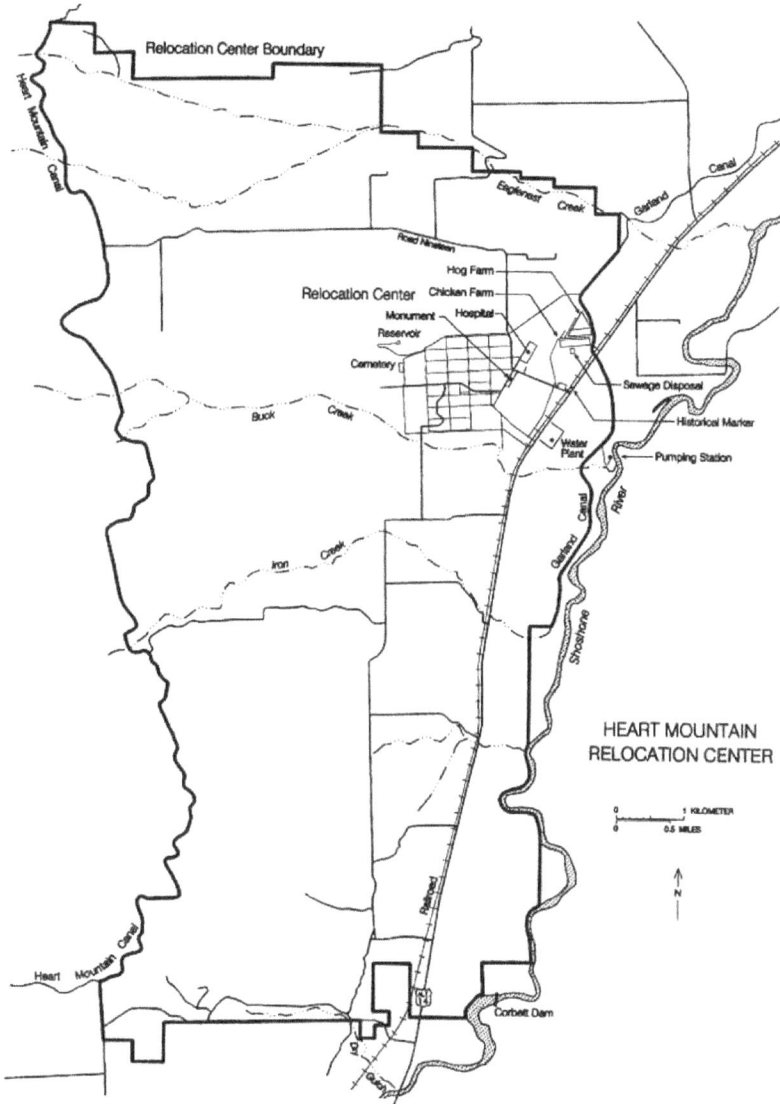

Figure 4.4: A map of Heart Mountain Relocation Center (Burton et al. Chapter 6).

With a more "permanent" situation, the government and the camps prisoners were making strides to make life a bit more routine and normal. It might be hard to imagine that one could find normalcy in a concentration camp, but, at the very least, they weren't going to be moved anymore, to the best of their knowledge anyway. In order to mentally cope, some sort of family life and routine must take place to not only survive but to thrive, and this is especially true for the Japanese family system.

"People lives were turned upside down. Some people that I knew didn't get to even come to the camps with their parents. A school friend of mine who was the same age as me (13) came to our camp with her 18-year-old sister. Because their parents were both schoolteachers, they were taken from their homes and put into a maximum security camp because their parents were consider a high threat. As I said, highly educated people were rounded up quickly, along with karate instructors, lawyers, and world travelers. These children were left to fend for themselves," says Nob somberly. "They had to sell all of their families' assets. They later found out that their parents, fearing the worst, had a secret storage space with all of their valuables, but the kids never knew about it. They, like all of the other families, lost everything."

Figure 4.5 George, Nob, and Shimayo

To help cope, the people filled their days with school, work, and activities, but, in what was one of the strangest turn of events of all, the camp not only allowed but encouraged the prisoners to form a government. The best guess is that this was done to avoid any uprising by making the Japanese feel that they had a voice, whether they truly did or not. Nob explains how it was presented:

> "The authorities said 'We're going to show you what democracy is about, you can do self governing and each block is going to elect a manager who will represent your wants and needs of the administration.' The managers selected a leader who passed on their requests and complaints to the proper authority. When the prisoners finally had their elections the camp said, 'We don't like the people you elected.' This is another instance where I could find humor in the situation. They elected second generations or Niseis as they are called in Japanese. They knew that Niseis would respect the first-generation Issei's elders and their wishes, not the plans of the camp's government. We were always civil even under

such duress. We stuck together with no fighting or bickering."

For children, their days were rather similar to their days before. They would attend school and make up games to play around the camp with the other kids, which landed them in trouble from time to time. One day Nob "squeezed between the wires" with some of his friends to chase a bunny into the brush simply because Nob thought it would be "cool to pet and play with." The guards in the tower, however, had less of a sense of humor about it.

> "The guard was blowing a whistle to get our attention from the tower as we were clearly outside of the camp now," laughs Nob. "Eventually a jeep pulled up with the sergeant of the guards to take us back. We saw him coming and all ducked down disappearing behind the sagebrush. The guard yelled, 'I know you guys are there and you better get back.' We scampered back after being yelled at by the MPs as well. Needless to say, we didn't mention it to our parents when we got home."

It was innocent fun but ended with a reminder that they are still prisoners of war. However, even with all of these potentially scary situations many of the children didn't mind says Nob:

> "Some of the kids that were really young actually liked the situation of the camps because their friends were so close. They were too young to have the understanding of the situation and their parents protected them from needing to know everything."

He even joked that of all the children, the ones whose parents were farmers liked the camps most because they no longer had to tend the fields after school, and their neighbor friends were closer than half a mile away, unlike back home.

Nob was at that tender age in which he was young enough to be a bit more flexible to the conditions of the situation but old enough to have the understanding that nothing would ever be the same again. The best activity, in his opinion, that made camp life feel a bit more normal was that Heart Mountain actually allowed the detainees children to form Boy Scout troops. This formed one of Nob's most powerful memories of the camp, which he talked about in striking detail with the broadest smile. He was so moved that they got to do what all other troops outside the prisoner camps did, including going camping. This must have seemed so ironic considering the circumstances.

> "Back in those days we had a lot of respect for society and that played a major role in the life of our camp," says Nob. "In the Japanese culture, character traits are very important, and here was an organization for kids that stressed character. They fit right into the camp and got a lot of support from the parents."

The parents were concerned that they no longer had a traditional type family because they were forced to live in barracks with other families, and they were no longer doing the simple family things like having a family dinner because they were made to have meals in the mess hall with 300 other people. Boy Scouts seemed to relieve their sense of losing all family values because it was an activity that encouraged values.

Figure 4.6 Photograph in Heart Mountain of the Shimokochi and Watanabe Families

However, mostly what the boys liked about it is that they got to do fun things. Besides camp meetings and camping, they also participated in the holiday celebrations. There would be a huge parade with the drum and bugle corps, and the Boy Scouts would march. Anytime they had some kind of a ceremony, whether it was the 4th of July, Memorial Day or a soldier was killed in action, the troops played some sort of role. There was competition among the seven troops. They had a setup or system of competition in which the troops that did the most activities got points along with merit badges, and they would even go camping in the summertime, earning even more points for that.

Figure 4.7 Belt, patches, and pin from Troop 333 Boy Scout Uniform

Nob grins like a little boy recalling one of his favorite camp stories:

> "Our Troop #333 took the district flag three out of four times, and we were proud of that. The thing is that we hardly had any Boy Scout equipment unlike today. It was a good thing actually because we had to carry it all by ourselves anyway and we had to walk every inch of the way. We used to camp along the Shoshone River. It was about a mile east of us (which was outside of the camp) and we'd pick up some food supply at the commissary. The people who worked there were pretty generous. We got meat, potatoes, onions, pancake flour along with honey for syrup. We would lie down on the banks of the river in our bedding but not all of us had sleeping bags although the campers just didn't care because we were

outside of the prison and just that alone made us feel good."

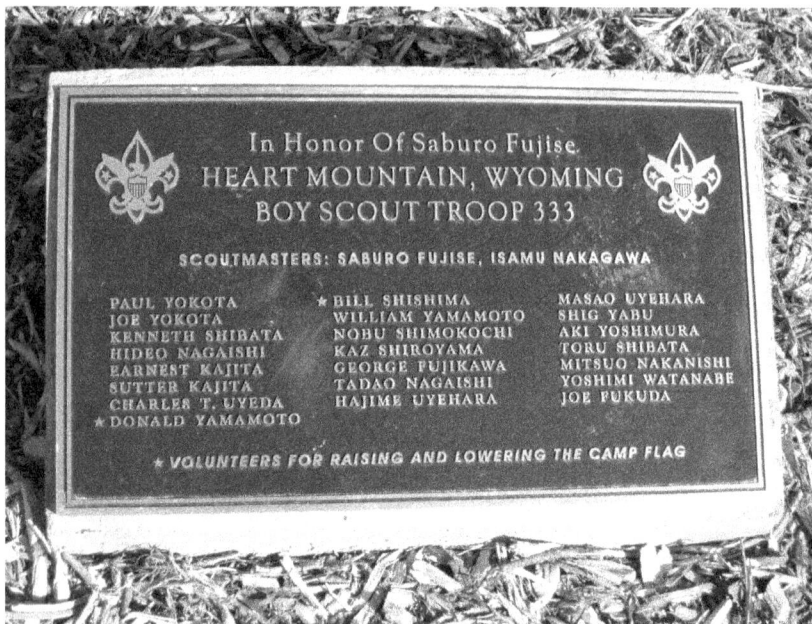

Figure 4.8 Photograph of plaque commemorating Boy Scout Troop 333

Nob talks about his scouting days with wonderment and pride:

"As we lay down at bed time you could look up at the stars, listen to the insects and frogs. We'd sing that Bing Crosby song, Don't Fence Me In:

'Oh, give me land, lots of land under starry skies above,
Don't fence me in.
Let me ride through the wide open country that I love,
Don't fence me in.
Let me be by myself in the evenin' breeze,
And listen to the murmur of the cottonwood trees,
Send me off forever but I ask you please,
Don't fence me in.

Just turn me loose, let me straddle my old saddle
Underneath the western skies.

On my Cayuse, let me wander over yonder
Till I see the mountains rise.

I want to ride to the ridge where the west commences
And gaze at the moon till I lose my senses
And I can't look at hobbles and I can't stand fences
Don't fence me in.

Oh, give me land, lots of land under starry skies,
Don't fence me in.
Let me ride through the wide open country that I love,
Don't fence me in.
Let me be by myself in the evenin' breeze
And listen to the murmur of the cottonwood trees
Send me off forever but I ask you please,
Don't fence me in

Just turn me loose, let me straddle my old saddle
Underneath the western skies
On my Cayuse, let me wander over yonder
Till I see the mountains rise.
Ba boo ba ba boo.

I want to ride to the ridge where the west commences
And gaze at the moon till I lose my senses
And I can't look at hobbles and I can't stand fences
Don't fence me in.
No.
Poppa, don't you fence me in.'
(music by Cole Porter, Lyrics by Robert Fletcher and
Cole Porter)

We had so much fun doing that and I described the
experience with so much affection that I got criticized
for making it sound like being incarcerated was so much
fun, but I don't think the camping experience would
have been as much fun if we were already free. This
tasted so much sweeter," Nob explains.

The biggest Boy Scout activity was the jamboree. All the troops got
together for some activities, competitions and they would all camp out

together. They invited other non-camp troops to join the jamboree and the Cody (Wyoming) troop came. Several of the Boy Scouts that Nob met have since become politicians. The few he could recall meeting personally were Alan Simpson, who was not interred but visited from the nearby Cody troop, and Norman Mineta, who, like Nob, was a resident of Heart Mountain. Nob wasn't close with either of them, as they were two years younger than he, but he remembers them specifically. Alan Simpson would later be elected to represent Wyoming in the U.S. Senate from 1979-1997 and now serves as a Chairman of the National Commission on Fiscal Responsibility and Reform. Norman Mineta was a judge in San Jose from 1971-1975 and a U.S. congressman representing California's 13 and 15th districts from 1975-1995. He worked for President Bill Clinton as Secretary of Commerce and for President George W. Bush as the Secretary of Transportation. Speaking of Mineta, Nob beams, "That's not bad. Once looked upon as an undesirable to the American way, imprisoned wrongfully and now he serves the very government that didn't trust him."

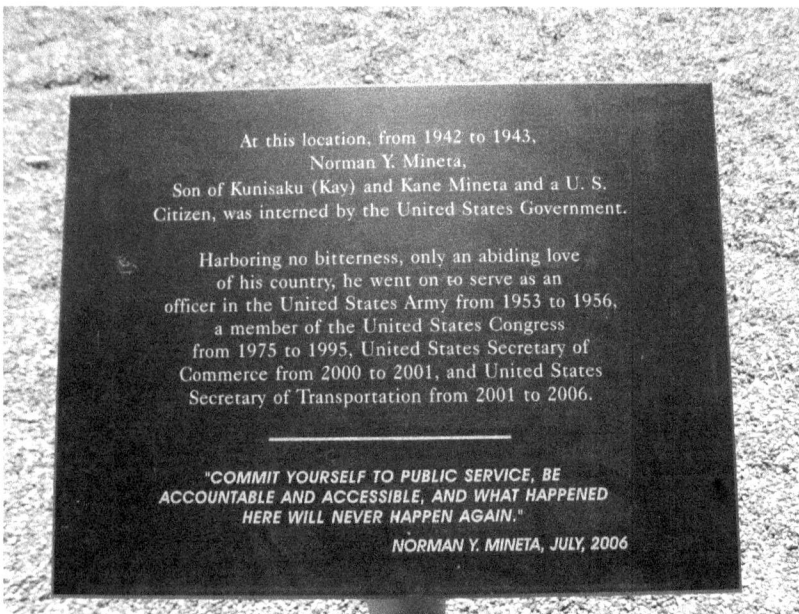

Figure 4.9 Plague at Heart Mountain Interpretative Learning Center

Even though scouting was Nob's favorite activity, there were many other things offered to the prisoners. Martial arts, sumo wrestling and dancing were popular, and the camp went so far as to hand out quizzes, crossword puzzles and word searches for pastime activities. But the most loved

activity by kids of high-school age were the social clubs (World War Two
– Japanese Internment Camps in the U.S.A).

> "A big morale booster was the athletic games. Baseball,
> softball and football which we played against teams
> outside of the camp were fun! Some of those teams came
> from over 100 miles away over treacherous roads. We
> won most of the games except basketball. The whites
> had a definite height advantage," laughs Nob.

While these activities were sanctioned by the camp, some were not, but
the people did what they could to pass the time, especially the kids. Block
29 was a guard tower and was near the Shimokochi's living quarters. Nob
shares a story about one afternoon when he and some other children
engaged a guard in a conversation.

> "He was telling us how he had limited service and
> mobility because of some physical problems. We offered
> to buy him an ice cream cone at the canteen. So he
> dropped us a few coins, and we ran to buy an ice cream
> cone. We didn't have any money so we couldn't buy a
> cone for ourselves, but we got one for him."

If you are waiting for the twist or the payoff of redemption in this story,
there isn't one. Nob simply found the story amusing from the standpoint
of the children being able to talk with the guard at all. It is also just
another reminder that kids are kids no matter what the circumstances.

Just as they did at Santa Anita, many people had jobs in the camp. Frankly
it was the only way that things could run well, if at all, but to be sure the
injustices seen at Santa Anita extended into this camp as well:

> "The internees worked at various jobs within the camp,
> but the WRA (War Relocation Authority) decided that
> the Japanese could not be paid more than a private could
> in the army, whose salary was $21 a month. Most jobs
> paid between $12 and $19 per month. Likewise,
> Japanese-American teachers were paid $228 a year
> although Caucasian instructors earned $2,000 per year
> and senior teachers were paid $2,600 annually...In

November 1942, Japanese American hospital workers walked out because of pay discrimination. Internee doctors were paid $19 per month, while Caucasian nurses working at the camp's hospital were paid $150 per month" (History – Life in Camp).

Nob's sister, Yuri, was able to leave the camps early and permanently to attend college, and she enrolled in an all-girl college in Missouri. This was largely due to the help of the Quakers, who, during this war and many others were instrumental in assisting those affected by war, along with the many other philanthropic endeavors they have engaged in since the origins of the church. Nob reveals why Yuri's leaving was bittersweet on many levels for his family:

"Of course we were going to miss her, but also we were poor as church mice, and she made money for the family by working in the mess hall. Therefore, it was difficult on the family to say goodbye to her and lose that additional income, but my father wouldn't hear of her turning down the opportunity. Education was very important to our family and the Japanese as whole, so we had no other options as far as we were concerned."

Her continuing education was going to be of further assistance to her integration into society, and it was important especially in light of the current circumstances. Nob is quick to reinforce the notion that all of these Japanese people fit and work perfectly in the American society and culture peacefully and quietly even after all of the injustices: "The belief is that we weren't capable of being assimilated because we were too different, but that simply wasn't true." Unbeknownst to Nob, the Japanese were going to soon get their chance to put that belief into action once again.

Chapter Five
Freedom!

Eventually the day finally came when the war was over, and the prisoners left Heart Mountain Internment Camp. It closed on November 10, 1945, with a peak population of 10,767. So it would seem obvious that the people would be rejoicing in the fact that they were going back home, but Nob recalls it quite differently:

> "The people on the West Coast said that they didn't want us back. They said, 'Don't come back or we'll kill you!'"

The government was putting a lot of pressure on the residents to get out of the camp, but the people were terrified because there was no place to go – no houses, no jobs and nobody in the area wanted them. The jobs and houses that were available were being given to the returning veterans, and the Japanese were simply outcasts. The government gave everyone $25 and a free train ticket to anywhere they wanted to go but reiterated to never ever come back to the West Coast.

Eventually, this exclusion order would be rescinded:

> "On December 17th, 1944 U.S. Major General Henry C. Pratt announced that beginning January 2nd, 1945, the federal government would officially end the exclusion order that prevented Japanese and Japanese-Americans from returning to the West Coast following their release from World War II internment camps. His announcement contributed to a fiery debate over Japanese and Japanese-American 'resettlement'—an idea that many…supported, but that also had strong opposition…" (Speidel).

However, just as the Civil Rights Act of 1964 didn't truly end segregation (even until this very day, some would argue), the ending of the exclusion order did very little to counteract all of the negative media and stereotypes that had been perpetuated by the United States government. The damage was done.

Everyone left the camps by train. When asked if the day he left the camp was a joyful day for him, Nob responded with mixed feelings:

> "Yes. But it was also difficult for me as a kid. We were parting from our friends, and we knew that we may never see them again because we were all displaced. I was able to give an address when many didn't, but I still lost contact with a lot of our friends."

The Shimokochi family specifically went to Billings, Montana, eventually headed eastward to Chicago and finally ended up in Cleveland. As Nob remembers:

> "My dad had a lead on a job for a rich family in the Cleveland area because his friend, Mr. Fukui, was working as a domestic servant at their home. Dad filled his position because when they opened up California once again to the Japanese Mr. Fukui wanted to re-establish his business as a mortician. This was risky considering that while it was legally open to the Japanese; the atmosphere was hostile at best. The fifth generation of Fukuis are still operating Fukui Mortuary, which is still open in Los Angeles, California, and is an invaluable part of the community" (fukuimortuary.com).

Nob's father worked as a domestic for one year before moving to Royal Oak, Michigan, in 1946. While he was grateful for the work, he didn't want to be a domestic for the rest of his life. He heard about a job at First Baptist Church in Royal Oak and decided "he would rather be working for God than this guy." (As a side note, the FBC in Royal Oak is still there as a historic building but is now Genesis the Church.) A Potter moving van came and got Nob's family. The Potters were members of the church and one of them eventually became the mayor of Royal Oak. The Shimokochis had finally found their home.

Once the family got settled in, Nob did what most people would find unthinkable: Nob joined the United States military at age 17 (with the signed permission of his parents). Why would a man whose entire family had been imprisoned for no reason whatsoever join the very military and country that wrongfully took all that he knew and changed his life forever?! With a look of determination and stern tone, Nob said his response was that "we were all accused of being spies and saboteurs, but we were very loyal to the United States." As children they didn't have an anti-American agenda and Nob wanted to prove it by joining the military. He wasn't the only one that felt that way, as pictured below. This monument is at Heart Mountain and honors more then 600 of its internees who left to serve in the U.S Armed Forces.

Figure 5.1 Photograph of plaque commemorating Heart Mountain military inductees

There was another reason that inspired Nob to enlist:

> "The guys in the 442nd Combat Team, their motto was 'go for broke' and even though they had a 300 percent casualty rate there fortitude was commendable. I was too young to be a part of that at camp. I was only 16 but we heard all of these glowing reports of their valor in the war and I wish I could have been a part of it. So when I got out of the camp and got old enough, I enlisted when I was 17 voluntarily."

His brother-in-law, Max Koga, fought with them as well:

> "Yuri's husband was in the 442nd combat team; in 1943
> they decided to draft the boys from the camps to fight in
> the Army 100th battalion. They were a Nisei battalion and
> existed from prewar in Hawaii, long before1941. A
> regiment normally consists of four battalions, but after
> Dec. 7th, they were stripped of their weapons and
> relegated to digging ditches and KP (Kitchen Patrol)
> work. After the government decided to conscript the
> Japanese, the 100th wanted to keep their identity. They
> became the 442nds 1st Battalion and were the most
> highly decorated regiment in the U.S. Army history,
> earning over 16,000 medals, including 21 medals of
> honor and 7 presidential citations. There also was the
> 552nd Artillery BN that freed the Dachau (first Nazi
> concentration camp opened in Germany) Extermination
> Camp."

However honor, allegiance or provocation in some cases weren't the only
reasons people joined the military. Some younger Japanese people had
nowhere to go or couldn't find a good source of income because of
overall prejudice or anti-Asian sentiment as a whole in the country.

> "It was rough all over. Families got split up and parents
> couldn't support all the kids so they would go to work as
> domestic servants until they finished high school. Some
> worked in agriculture," says Nob. "My friend went out
> and picked beans because that was the only job available
> and it put food on the table. It was back breaking work
> and it took hours just to fill a one bushel basket and load
> it onto a truck. Even after it was far too heavy to
> continue carrying the man with the truck would say,
> 'Those aren't enough beans' and he would continue to
> pick. At the end of the day he would make three bucks."

So, encouraged by grim stories told by his friends, Nob opted for the
Army 7th Infantry Division MI (military intelligence) unit in Korea. Nob
refers to his division as "red hour" or "h-hour", which is taken from the
logo: a red circle with a black hour glass that was formed by the letter

seven printed side by side with an inverted one. "During the war, the Japanese were not allowed to join the Air Force or Navy," says Nob. Many soldiers during this time frame were allowed to join the armed forces but most were not allowed to assume a role of combat.

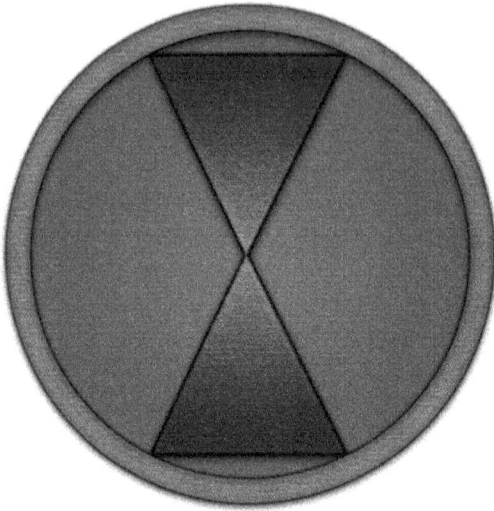

Figure 5.2 Image of Army 7th Infantry logo

They sent Nob to the 38th parallel as part of the 317th Headquarters Intelligence. The 38th parallel was a popular name given to latitude 38° N that in East Asia roughly demarcates North Korea and South Korea. The line was chosen by U.S. military planners at the Potsdam Conference (July 1945) near the end of World War II as an army boundary, north of which the U.S.S.R. was to accept the surrender of the Japanese forces in Korea and south of which the Americans were to accept the Japanese surrender. The line was intended as a temporary division of the country…" (38th Parallel).

There were a lot of North Koreans trying to escape to South Korea. This was the location of refugee camps where they stayed temporarily, and Nob had to interrogate its inhabitants for military information.

"We collected a lot the intelligence about the North Korean army and the position of the units, even about where the regiments and division head quarters were," Nob recalls. "We knew all of that and in some cases we knew who the officers were. They gave up diagrams of the towns and specific location of the military. We had a huge map on the wall with these colored pins marking all the units. We had a curtain over it and would slide it back whenever we looked at it."

Nob, with a coy grin, talks about a certain spy who made her way into their office:

"There was a spy that got access to our space and we didn't know she was a spy, and since she was Japanese, we got kind of friendly with her. She said she wanted some stationary to write some notes under the premise that the insignia on the stationary is of the crack 7th Division. She was writing about not being able to see the maps because it was closed off by the curtain. This made us look good because it was military policy. She was telling how she knew each of our names and how once in a while they got to talk to their families at home. She never gained access to any useful information that we were aware of, and CIC (Counterintelligence Corps) had her boxed in. As it turned out, the letter to her boss was given to a courier, and it got intercepted."

He doesn't know what exactly happened to her but one could assume that it probably didn't end very favorably.

War is never easy for anyone, and it wasn't lost on many that large groups of Japanese men were in charge of interrogating other Asians. Nob just saw it as part of his job for the betterment of democracy and his own personal safety:

"Well the Koreans hated us so that helped. Their language did have the same vowel tones and the intonation was similar to Japanese but we couldn't understand a word. But since their country had been occupied by Japan for 40 years, they all understood Japanese. Either way, it was important for us to do our jobs regardless of however we personally felt."

This certainly made their jobs difficult, but it didn't detour them or keep them for doing a great job. Just when Nob had just about enough of his service time, he was given an out.

"In 1949 President Truman decided to pull us out of Korea, and they asked me, 'Would you like to finish your enlistment or get out?' I knew the war was coming. I mean it was the entire reason why we were obtaining intelligence and I was happy to have come home vertically, so I left. When you enlist you've got to understand it may be peace time today and war time tomorrow. I got out while I still could. I was lucky….it was God's blessing."

While still enlisted in the service, Nob traveled back to Hiroshima. He knew that his family was in very rough shape there, and because the economy was crushed thoroughly, he wanted to bring them gifts to lift their spirits and bring them some joy.

"For my grandfather I bought a moleskin coat with a sheared sheepskin lining," says Nob. "I wanted to lift everyone's spirits. Maybe even my own…besides being put into a camp, I suffered some loss from the Nuclear bombing in Hiroshima; a cousin of mine was fried by that bomb!"

He showed up as a Japanese man in an American military uniform. What a strange sight that must have been to see. While it wasn't entire unique, it also wasn't commonplace, especially in Hiroshima. The plane flew him to Tokyo, and he took a few trains to Hiroshima, which actually is a delta that literally translates as "wide island" (Hiroshima).

"Australian troops were occupying that part of the country," says Nob. "Me in my uniform traveling through Japanese land that was being occupied by Aussies in their uniform was astonishing to fathom. The train ride was free and a dollar charge for a sleeper car and when I got close to my destination the porter came and woke me up."

At this time in the era of transportation and especially because there was so much structural damage done to the region because of the war, there was no easy, direct route into the city.

"I caught a freight train to Seno when they told me, 'This is where you get off,'" he laughs. "I pulled out a piece of paper with my grandparents' address on it and asked, 'Where is this house?' In rapid-fire fashion the man replied, 'Well you go down this road, take the right fork, go over this bridge and so on.'"

Figure 5.3 Image of Google map of the route from Seno to Hiroshima

Meanwhile, Nob was not only confused by the directions but was managing to get more and more lost until he had an encounter that he could have never have imagined. "Shortly after wandering around for a bit, there was a guy with a bike walking, and he told me that he's my uncle." Nob tossed his duffle bag on his bike, and they both walked back to Nob's grandfather's house. Nob is quick to point out, "I couldn't have walked very far with that extremely heavy duffle bag, so I'm glad that he showed up when he did!" His grandfather told Nob's Uncle Itsuichi that Nob was planning to arrive in Hiroshima City that day, so he thought it was safe to assume that the Japanese man wearing an American military uniform was indeed Nob.

As was customary at the time, there was a hot bath awaiting Nob:

> "Baths were not used to clean your self in but to relax. You were expected to wash up first since multiple people would use the same bath water. You could compare it to a modern day hot tub. Since it was manually heated from below and water had to be brought in, it made for a lot of work and was therefore a luxury. This bathwater was so hot I could barely dip my foot in up to my ankle!"

Figure 5.4 Photo of Risaku Shimokochis home in Japan.

After a soak and a much needed visit with his family, he made his way back stateside to continue on with his life and part of that meant completing his time as a soldier.

76

"I had two weeks vacation, so I hurried back to Tokyo only to find that I couldn't fly back to Korea. I was only a staff sergeant off duty and had no priority. I walked to the General of the Army (five-star) MacArthur's headquarters. He was also known as "SCAP", Supreme Commander Allied Powers, a name he was proud of. A guard told me to make myself scarce since, 'MacArthur is coming!!' and I was curious, so I hid behind the huge stone pillars of the Dai-Ichi building. All pedestrian and vehicular traffic was stopped. A jeep with screaming sirens and a machine gun manned by an officer came roaring in: one jeep in front and one behind a black Packard sedan. The guard opens the door and out comes the general. He receives a snappy salute, and the general returns a soft sloppy one. This was standard army protocol."

There were many memories that stayed with Nob long after the war ended and kept coming back into his life in the most unexpected ways. Nob's intelligence force operations, Sergeant Haruo Sasaki, was a career man. While the rest of the troops came and went, Haruo stayed until the end of their intelligence mission when the government finally pulled him out sending him to Japan. He was valuable because he knew the Korean army so well, but it was his time to go onto something else. Nob shares a very unusual twist of fate story about his Sergeant:

"When the Korean War started, I saw a newspaper article that said they were sending a bunch of war correspondence to Korea and it crashed. My operations sergeant was on that plane and the only survivor. I hadn't seen him in 30 years at least when my wife and I were visiting her cousin in Sacramento. We were sitting at a restaurant, and I randomly asked his wife's cousin's husband, 'Does anyone know a guy named Haruo Sasaki?' And her husband said, 'He's my golfing buddy of mine, why don't we invite him for dinner tomorrow?'"

Nob loved the idea of seeing him again, especially as a civilian:

"We had a really nice chat, and I told him that I read the article about him and never heard a single thing again! He said that he was flying out of Tokyo and it wasn't too far out before there was an explosion. The next thing he knew was that he was falling out of the sky and could even see the red flasher on the belly of the plane as he was dropping like a rock heading for the open water. He was falling fast but finally was able to pull the rip cord on his parachute and safely floated down to eventually hit the water. His parachute started to fill with water and drag him down, so he pulled a pin to release his inflatable vest called a Mae West. Unfortunately he couldn't swim but saw a yellow raft floating in the water that apparently fell from the plane. He dog-paddled to the raft and bobbed around in it for eight to ten hours before some Japanese fishermen scooped him out of the water. When he went home, the Air Force sent a couple of lieutenants to debrief him. They talked to him like he had something to do with the explosion, so he asked them to leave! Why would a guy who dedicated his life to military do that, especially considering he was on the plane as well?!" says Nob exasperatedly.

Chapter Six
Onward

After leaving the military, Nob went back to Royal Oak, moved in with his family and finished high school at the age of 21. During this time he met his wife to be: Anna Nitta (born March in 1933). Her father was an old friend of Nob's father, George, and her family used to come over to Nob's family's house on the West Coast in the early 1900s.

> "My dad kept drifting down south, and on his way to Los Angeles, he worked a few jobs. Sorting logs, doing some farm work, but he did not care for farming. Anna's father became a farmer at Loomis, near Sacramento, in fruit and berry country. The area produced peaches, plums and apricots and even strawberries. I remember my dad used to always write letters to him, and I always wondered who he was."

When the war ended, Anna's dad moved to the Monroe, Michigan, area and eventually transferred to Birmingham, Michigan. He eventually died, and Nob's father invited to stay with them, but Nob was off in the military at the time. When he returned, the Nitta family had bought a little home in Detroit and no longer lived with his family, but they were all still very close. Since Nob was pretty much a stranger in town, he started hanging out with Clarence, Anna's brother, and Nob immediately noticed that Clarence had a pretty little sister. He ended up dating her, and a few years later, they married. They wed on August 15, 1953. (It is worth noting that Anna was also in an internment camp: Tule Lake.)

Nob and his new bride were married at the church his father worked for, First Baptist Church of Royal Oak, and the wedding was officiated by Pastor Woodrow Clark. They had a reception in the fellowship hall that exists in the church to this very day. They started their life together living with Nob's parents, and then did what most young couples did, which was rent a small flat. Finally, they bought a home in Royal Oak, Michigan, in 1957. Nob states it was intended only to be their first house, but 55 years later they are still there. That was the year his first son, David, was born. He arrived a month after they moved in. "I had a $4000 nest egg I saved during my military days, and the home cost around $14,000. My how times are different."

With all of this good fortune, there were some sour notes along the way:

"When my son David was two and Ken was one, I was diagnosed with cancer. The doctors told me not to have any more children because I was expected to die, but I clearly survived, and five years later Anna got pregnant with Susan. You can't get stuck on bad news. There is a lesson in that."

His life went forward, and he is still around to watch his kids with their kids grow and thrive.

Nob has taken advantage of many opportunities to learn as much as he can about his heritage, as have some of his grandchildren:

"In 1999 I went to Japan for a visit. I bought a bunch of books from Borders bookstore and studied the vocabulary. I was there in 1949, but I wanted to go back some day, and it was over 50 years since then. I would have liked to have gone back with my wife, but she didn't want to go. Unless I went myself, I would never get there. So, I went back and established a relationship with some relatives, and I met a second cousin, Yuko Heya; she had an interest in the U.S., and she figured this is her chance, so we talked on the phone every now and then. Phone rates were very expensive in Japan at the time. Eventually she came to visit us in the states a couple of times and got to meet Susan's family. Annie, my granddaughter, ended up going to Japan in the summer of 2012. Last couple days of their visit to Japan, they had some free time in Hiroshima. They were able to meet there at the peace memorial park and the hotel there. They had dinner together with the group. Yuko has a younger sister who had a daughter a year older than Annie. She was going to a university in Tokyo and wanted to meet Annie. So she took the bullet train down to Hiroshima, and they got together. Annie had a hard time communicating because she doesn't speak much Japanese and her friend didn't speak much English but they established a relationship. I guess somewhere in that museum is my cousin's jacket."

On Top of Heart Mountain
June 1999

Figure 6.1 Photo of Nob at Heart Mountain

In 2011 Nob went back to Heart Mountain Grand Opening of the Interpretative Learning Center.

HEART MOUNTAIN RELOCATION CENTER
HAS BEEN DESIGNATED A
NATIONAL HISTORIC LANDMARK

BETWEEN 1942 AND 1945, GUARD TOWERS AND BARBED WIRE FENCES ON THIS SITE CONFINED A COMMUNITY OF NEARLY 11,000 FORCIBLY UPROOTED PEOPLE OF JAPANESE ANCESTRY, MOST OF WHOM WERE AMERICAN CITIZENS. ALL WERE VICTIMS OF RACIAL PREJUDICE, WARTIME HYSTERIA, AND FAILED POLITICAL LEADERSHIP.

THIS SITE POSSESSES NATIONAL SIGNIFICANCE IN ILLUSTRATING THE HISTORY OF THE UNITED STATES OF AMERICA
2006
NATIONAL PARK SERVICE
UNITED STATES DEPARTMENT OF THE INTERIOR

Figure 6.2 Plaque commemorating Heart Mountain as a National Historic Landmark

Figure 6.3 Heart Mountain Sign

Figure 6.4 Photograph of Ruby Nitta and Nob at Heart Mountain

Chapter Seven
Happy Endings

Figure 7.1 Nob on his 83rd birthday

"There aren't many of my generation, the Nisei, still living," says Nob, who is now 84. (His sister, Yuri, passed in 2009 at age 85). "Many of my generation didn't feel the impact of the camps like their parents did because they were either conscripted into service or were too young and felt it to be more like a getaway or camping." After having gone to a dedication of a museum at Heart Mountain, Nob reflected on what he wanted his legacy to be and replied without hesitation:

> "To raise good children. I came here starting from zero
> and raised three kids; two boys and a girl. They all
> became engineers but more importantly they turned out
> to be very nice, kind, loving people and that's my pride."

Everyone wants to raise good kids, but it brings a special kind of honor for a man of Japanese descent to have children who bring the family honor.

Nob's children are David Kiyoshi, who was born in 1957, and has two sons, Nick and Dan; Ken Noboru, who was born December in 1958, and has one daughter, Kathryn; and Susan Anne, who was born in 1963, and has a son and daughter, Annie and Jimmy. Nob beams with pride, while he is being interviewed about his children. He is so grateful that his children

"are so good to me. Ken, my second son, he loves to help people. Not only that, but he has a talent to make, repair, and create things. Electric, plumbing, carpentry, auto skills, you name it. He is able and willing to help a lot of different people. I can call Ken anytime. Dave is very intelligent, hard working and driven. His work keeps him from spending a ton of time with the family, but they all show in their own way their love for the family. He is a very important man, and I respect that. Susan was one of these kids who did what she was told. We had no problem disciplining her. She was just a good kid but very shy and quiet. While she is still shy and quiet, she has come into her own. After graduating college she had to become very extroverted. I used to worry about her shyness. But she has a good life…married with kids. Her kids are brilliant with school. That's of course a joy for me. She's always doing things for me, buying me things she thinks might be of a help to me and her mom. Little flash lights, clothes, etc… However the day to day phone calls are for mom. She took me to Wyoming for the trip back to Heart Mountain. I needed her on that trip and she knew it! I was going to go alone but she would have none of it and that's what good kids do."

Figure 7.2 Anna, Annie, Jimmy, Sue, Nob

Figure 7.3 Great-grandson Kaelen and Nob

It is heartwarming and charming to watch Nob as he veers off topic and simply beams with pride to talk about his grandkids saying, "My grandkids are the best!" Musical and scholastic accomplishments are the crux of the conversation, and if I let him go on talking, our entire interviews would be all about them.

Figure 7.4 Photograph of Nob's Family in June 2011

Front: Susan Latos, Nancy Gdowski, Ken Shimokochi

Middle: Kathryn Shimokochi, Christina and Nick Shimokochi (with Kaelen in his lap), Dan Shimokochi, Nob Shimokochi
Back: Frank Latos, David Shimokochi, Anna Shimokochi, Anna (Annie) Latos, Jimmy Latos

Nob loves his children and feels it's important that they know not only where they've come from, but at what cost:

> "I was talking to my son, and he is fully integrated into society, but I reminded him that things are like this today because a lot of people died for it. You see, at the end of WWII, Japan was literally reduced to rubble and ash. All the able-bodied men went off to the battlefields, and very few returned. The civilian population suffered huge losses to the wall to wall incendiary nature of the nuclear bombs. The situation was desperate, but the survivors still had hope. They had that 'Gaman' and 'Gambaru' spirit: the mental toughness and resolve to endure the pain and discomfort. They made huge sacrifices and sent their children through the universities. Their Gross Domestic Product was only second to the U.S., while other WWII participants languished in near poverty even

after they benefited from the U.S.'s generous Marshall Plan (ERP or European Recovery Program). Japan's character traits were the same that were instilled into the Nisei generation. They helped us to emerge from nothing, and we were able to raise three children who are engineers that we are very proud of. "

In the end, Nob wanted to make the point that your circumstances do not define who you are. The reason for this book was to present proof that through perseverance, hard work, and a deep faith in God, he was able to overcome adversity. His heritage and family taught him that above all else, doing the right thing is always the important thing. Nob was able to rise above it all and raise a lovely family. He feels that his strong bond and the loving relationship he has with his family, church, and God is proof that we are not where we came from but a manifest of our heart, our faith and our culture. Nob went from prison to patriot but neither defined him. In the end, it was his heart and wonderment for what could be that ended up being his legacy.

Appendix – List of camps

Amache (Granada), CO
Opened August 24, 1942
Closed October 15, 1945
Peak population: 7,318

Gila River, AZ
Opened July 20, 1942
Closed November 10, 1945
Peak population: 13,348

Heart Mountain, WY
Opened August 12, 1942
Closed November 10, 1945
Peak population: 10,767

Jerome, AR
Opened October 6, 1942
Closed June 30, 1944
Peak population: 8,497

Manzanar, CA
Opened March 21, 1942
Closed November 21, 1945
Peak population: 10,046

Minidoka, ID
Opened August 10, 1942
Closed October 28, 1945
Peak population: 9,397

Poston, AZ
Opened May 8, 1942
Closed November 28, 1945
Peak population: 17,814

Rohwer, AR
Opened September 18, 1942
Closed November 30, 1945
Peak population: 8,475

Topaz, UT
Opened September 11, 1942
Closed October 31, 1945
Peak population: 8,130

Tule Lake, CA
Opened May 27, 1942
Closed March 20, 1946
Peak population: 18,789

References

"38th Parallel." Web. 14 February 2013.
<http://www.britannica.com/EBchecked/topic/592578/38th-parallel>

"Authorities: 'Balloon boy' Incident was a Hoax." 19 Oct. 2009. Web. 30 March. 2013.
<http://www.cnn.com/2009/US/10/18/colorado.balloon.investigation/index.html>

Burton, J., M. Farrell, F. Lord, and R. Lord. "Chapter 1." *Confinement and Ethnicity: An Overview of World War II Japanese American Relocation Sites.* 1 Sept. 2000. Web. 4 Jan. 2013.
<http://www.nps.gov/history/history/online_books/anthropology74/ce1.htm>3

Burton, J., M. Farrell, F. Lord, and R. Lord. "Chapter 6." *Confinement and Ethnicity: An Overview of World War II Japanese American Relocation Sites.* 1 Sept. 2000. Web. 4 Jan. 2013.
<http://www.cr.nps.gov/history/online_books/anthropology74/ce6.htm>

"Civil Rights: Japanese Americans, Minorities." Web. 4 April 2012.
<http://www.pbs.org/thewar/at_home_civil_rights_japanese_american.htm>

DeWitt, J.L. 1943. *Final Report; Japanese Evacuation from the West Coast 1942.* Washington D.C.: Govt. Printing Office.

Eleni. "Japanese American Internment Camps." Web. 10 October 2012.
http://www.ptla.us/Period7/EleniC.html

"Fukui Mortuary." Web. 3 Sept. 2012.
<http://www.fukuimortuary.com/fh/aboutus/history.cfm?&fh_id=10203>

"George Takei Biography." Web. 2 January 2013.
<http://www.georgetakei.com/bio.asp>

Havey, Lili. "Colorado State Archives Amache Internment Camp Watercolors by Lily Havey." Web. 24 June 2012.
<http://www.colorado.gov/dpa/doit/archives/wwcod/amache/Lily_Havey.html>

"H.R. 1540 (112th): National Defense Authorization Act for Fiscal Year 2012." Web. 10 January 2013.
<http://www.govtrack.us/congress/bills/112/hr1540>

"Hepburn Romanization." *Judopedia*. 9 September 2011.
        <http://judopedia.com/index.php?
        title=Hepburn_romanization>

Hersey, John. 1988. "Behind Barbed Wire." New York: *The New York*
        Times Magazine. 11 Sept.
        1988.<http://www.nytimes.com/1988/09/11/magazine/behind
        -barbed-wire.html?pagewanted=all&src=pm>

"Hiroshima." Web. 10 January
        2013.<http://www.hiroshimajohoku.ed.jp/school/english/index
        .html>

"Historical Timeline: History of Legal and Illegal Immigration to the
        United States." Web. 10 October 2012.
        <http://immigration.procon.org/view.resource.php?
        resourceID=002690##4>

"History – Life in Camp." Web. 7 Jan.
        2013.<http://heartmountain.org/history.html>

"Japanese-American Internment Camps." Web. 11 Feb. 2013.
        <http://www.bookmice.net/darkchilde/japan/camp.html>

"Japanese American Interment in World War 2." Web. 10 October 2012.
        http://www.freeinfosociety.com/article.php?id=10

"Leaving Home." *Japanese-Americans: The War at Home*. Web. 11 Feb. 2013.
        <http://teacher.scholastic.com/activities/wwii/ahf/mineta/leavi
        ng.htm>

Mackey, Mike. "A Brief History of the Heart Mountain Relocation Center
        and the Japanese American Experience." Web. 11 Feb. 2013.
        <http://www.english.illinois.edu/maps/poets/g_l/haiku/macke
        y.htm>

Norman, William. "Japanese Law and Culture on Inheritance with the
        Oldest Son." Web. 11 Nov. 2012.
        <http://www.ehow.com/facts_6870200_japanese-culture-
        inheritance-oldest-son.html>

Norton, Henry Kittredge. 1924. *The Story of California from the Earliest Days to the Present,*
7th ed. Chicago: A.C. McClurg.

Personal Justice Denied. 1982. U.S. Government.<http://www.archives.gov/research/japanese-americans/justice-denied/chapter-5.pdf>

"Santa Anita (detention facility)." *Densho Encyclopedia.* Densho. 17 March 2012. Web. 12 December 2012. <http://encyclopedia.densho.org/Santa%20Anita %20%28detention%20facility%29/>

"Santa Anita Park." Web. 10 Feb. 2013.<http://www.followhorseracing.com/en/races/tracks/s/santa-anita-park/>

"Santa Anita Park." *Wikipedia: The Free Encyclopedia.* Wikimedia Foundation, Inc. Web. 10 Feb. 2013. <http://en.wikipedia.org/wiki/Santa_Anita_Park>

Siasoco, Ricco Villanueva, and Shmuel Ross. "Japanese Relocation Centers." Web. 10 Dec. 2013. <http://www.infoplease.com/spot/internment1.html/>

Speidel, Jennifer. "After Internment: Seattle's Debate over Japanese Americans' Right to Return Home." Web. 13 Dec. 2012. <http://depts.washington.edu/civilr/after_internment.htm>

"The Chinese Experience in 19th Century America." Web. 13 Dec. 2012. <http://teachingresources.atlas.uiuc.edu/chinese_exp/introduction04.html>

"The History and Traditions of Sumo." Web.3 September 2012. <http://www.sumotalk.com/history.htm>

"World War Two – Japanese Internment Camps in the U.S.A." 25 February 2013. Web. 5 Jan. 2013. <http://www.historyonthenet.com/WW2/japan_internment_camps.htm>